I0439017

A Catalog of Graphic Symbols Used at Maintenance Control Centers: Toward a Symbol Standardization Process

Vicki Ahlstrom, ACT-530/ACB-220

Robert Muldoon, Northrop Grumman Information Technology

April 2002

DOT/FAA/CT-TN02/12

Document is available to the public
through the National Technical Information
Service, Springfield, Virginia 22161

U.S. Department of Transportation
Federal Aviation Administration

William J. Hughes Technical Center
Atlantic City International Airport, NJ 08405

NOTICE

This document is disseminated under the sponsorship of the U.S. Department of Transportation in the interest of information exchange. The United States Government assumes no liability for the contents or use thereof.

The United States Government does not endorse products or manufacturers. Trade or manufacturers' names appear herein solely because they are considered essential to the objective of this report.

1. Report No. DOT/FAA/CT-TN02/12	2. Government Accession No.	3. Recipient's Catalog No.	
4. Title and Subtitle A Catalog of Graphic Symbols Used at Maintenance Control Centers: Toward a Symbol Standardization Process		5. Report Date April 2002	
		6. Performing Organization Code ACT-530/ACB-220	
7. Author(s) Vicki Ahlstrom, ACT-530/ACB-220 and Robert Muldoon, Northrop Grumman Information Technology		8. Performing Organization Report No. DOT/FAA/CT-TN02/12	
9. Performing Organization Name and Address Federal Aviation Administration William J. Hughes Technical Center Atlantic City International Airport, NJ 08405		10. Work Unit No. (TRAIS)	
		11. Contract or Grant No.	
12. Sponsoring Agency Name and Address Federal Aviation Administration Human Factors Division 800 Independence Ave., S.W. Washington, DC 20591		13. Type of Report and Period Covered Technical Note	
		14. Sponsoring Agency Code AAR-100	

15. Supplementary Notes

16. Abstract

This document catalogs the symbols presented with the various interfaces used by Federal Aviation Administration Airway Facilities specialists. It includes a high-level overview of each system and the symbols and coding conventions used. These data were collected through analysis of software specifications, computer-based instruction manuals, and field site visits. The visits to field sites allowed verification of information from other sources and provided information about the environments that can affect the discrimination of visual symbols. Researchers used the information from the Human Factors Design Guide, International Organization for Standardization standards, and other sources to provide recommendations for visual symbols. The researchers used this information to evaluate the symbols used at Maintenance Control Centers, taking into consideration the observed environmental conditions, and provided recommendations toward a goal of symbol standardization.

17. Key Words Human Computer Interaction Symbol Attributes Symbol Design		18. Distribution Statement This document is available to the public through the National Technical Information Service, Springfield, Virginia, 22161.	
19. Security Classif. (of this report) Unclassified	20. Security Classif. (of this page) Unclassified	21. No. of Pages 93	22. Price

Form DOT F 1700.7 (8-72)   Reproduction of completed page authorized

Acknowledgments

The Office of the Chief Scientific and Technical Advisor for Human Factors, AAR-100 sponsored this work. The authors would like to thank Paul Krois from AAR-100 and Beverly Clark from AOP-30 whose valuable input made this effort possible. We would also like to thank Ray Sorise who gave us access to the information from computer-based instruction manuals and Mariann Abbonizio for helping with the literature review. We also would like to thank the individuals at the various sites who allowed us to observe systems in use, and the dozens of other people who provided information on various systems, symbols, and coding, but whose names escape us at this time or who wish to remain anonymous.

Table of Contents

List of Illustrations

List of Illustrations (Con't.)

Executive Summary

Airway Facilities (AF) is responsible for monitoring and controlling many different systems and equipment. Many of the interfaces used by AF specialists rely on visual symbols to represent objects and functions on a monitor. As new systems have been added over the years, the number of visual symbols to which the AF specialists are exposed has increased. It is difficult to determine the extent to which human factors was used in the design of the visual symbols used by these different systems. In addition, many of the visual symbols have been designed disregarding the environment as a whole. In other words, visual symbols for new systems are often introduced with little consideration to the other symbols that are already present in that environment or the environmental conditions as a whole. This practice leads to a proliferation of different visual symbols and coding methods presented in a single environment, taxing user memory and increasing the potential for error.

The purpose of this document was to collect information on the visual symbols currently used in the AF environment. It takes an integrated approach by looking across systems rather than within a single system and also identifying factors in the AF environment that can impact the design of visual symbols. Additionally, this document provides relevant human factors guidance against which the current visual symbols are compared.

A research team from the National Airspace System Human Factors Group (ACT-530/ACB-220) of the William J. Hughes Technical Center collected data through site visits to six facilities (four Air Route Traffic Control Center Maintenance Control Centers (MCCs) and two General Maintenance Control Centers). The research team reviewed computer-based instruction compact disks on various systems, interacted with subject matter experts, and studied software documentation manuals. These data provided information on the symbols used by 16 different systems, their meaning, and some of the coding conventions. The site visits also provided general information about the operational environments such as estimated viewing distances, ambient lighting, and number of systems in a work area.

This study identified and cataloged more than 200 unique visual symbols in use at the MCCs. Some of these symbols were used to encode status, some as object symbols that could be opened and manipulated, and some were used as part of graphic menus (also called toolbars or palettes). There were a few systems that used text pushbuttons rather than graphics. Overall, the systems, when viewed as a whole, showed a great deal of inconsistency in how information was represented to the users. The degree of fidelity used to represent graphic items on systems that used symbols also varied greatly from system to system.

The research team examined the systems for commonalities in function, objects, or concepts. Several commonalities were identified, including the PRINT function, the CPU object, and the concepts of CONFIGURE and ALARM. The researchers examined the way the systems conveyed these concepts to the users. They identified several inconsistencies. There were several ways in which the information differed between systems. In some cases, different graphics conveyed the same concept. In other cases, a graphic of one object (i.e., telephone) conveyed different meanings. Some concepts were conveyed graphically in one system and textually or through coding (i.e., color or shape) in another. This report presents examples of each of these items extracted from the AF system symbols.

This study is a first step toward standardization, but additional work needs to be done for symbol standardization to be successful. In many cases, the symbols are referred to by different terms. Human factors experts need to work with users to determine which of these terms are synonymous. It is also not yet known if any of the symbols have strong familiarity effects, such that the users associate particular meanings so strongly with a particular graphic that it is difficult to relearn. Additionally, this study did not look at comprehensibility for any of the symbols. Additional research should be conducted to provide the answers to these questions.

As a result of this study, we present several suggestions. We recommend that the overall number of symbols be decreased, where possible, through standardizing symbols across systems. To accomplish standardization, we recommend that human factors experts, together with AF users and other technical experts, work to further identify commonalities in function, objects, and concepts that are represented by the symbols and coding conventions contained in this document. We recommend that these parties come to an agreement on the level of realism and style that will be used for graphic symbols on AF systems, ensuring that any agreement complies with the human factors guidance contained within this document. We also recommend that any proposed standardized symbols be tested against existing symbols for comprehensibility.

Relevant human factors guidelines are contained within this document, along with an initial set of common functions, objects, and concepts. We recommend that the guidelines presented in this document be used to set a framework bounding the solutions proposed in a standardization effort.

The information contained in this report can also be used as a "lessons learned" of sorts. It underscores the need to take an integrated approach in system design, taking into account existing symbols and coding conventions when designing a new product. This report highlights cases where tenets of consistency have been violated and gives suggestions based on human factors research and guidelines on how to design effective symbols. Thus, this report can be used not only toward AF symbol standardization but also as information for future symbol development.

1. INTRODUCTION

The Federal Aviation Administration (FAA) is planning to increase the number of systems remotely monitored and controlled. When a system is remotely monitored or controlled, the status and other important information are often represented to the user as an alphanumeric or pictorial symbol on a display screen. Airway Facilities (AF) is responsible for many different systems created by different organizations, therefore, the AF specialists who monitor and control the systems will encounter an increasing variety of visual symbols. To minimize confusion and errors, symbols should be well designed and should take into consideration the other symbols that exist in the same operational area, the physical environment as a whole, and pre-established meanings for symbols.

One method of maximizing effective symbol use while minimizing confusion between symbols is to standardize symbols used to represent information necessary to monitor these systems (Ahlstrom, Cranston, Mogford, Ramakrishnan, & Birt, 1998). There is currently an effort underway by AF to improve the way information is represented through standardization. In order for this effort to be successful, information must be gathered on current visual symbols and the environments in which they are used. Human factors knowledge from the literature and guidelines documents should be applied to provide recommendations on what makes symbols effective. Researchers from the National Airspace System (NAS) Human Factors Branch (ACT-530/ACB-220) of the William J. Hughes Technical Center (WJHTC) have been asked to help with this effort by cataloging and documenting symbols currently in use and providing human factors recommendations for symbols.

1.1 Background

Visual symbols are pictorial representations that stand for or suggest something else. Although visual symbols displayed on computer screens are often referred to as icons, for the purposes of this paper, researchers will use the term "symbol" throughout this document. Symbols displayed on computers fall under different categories: some symbols represent a pointer or cursor, some symbols represent objects on maps, some show the status of items they are representing, and others represent objects as a means of interacting with the system.

The use of symbols in computer systems has become progressively more common. With the increase in computerized equipment over the last decade, AF specialists are exposed to more and more different symbols. This document presents information on the current use of visual symbols on AF computers, their appearance, and guidance on effective symbol design.

Symbol use

AF equipment and systems use symbols for many different reasons, mainly for the advantages they provide over text displays. Symbols can save space, speed visual search, and facilitate recognition and recall (Horton, 1994). Research has shown that well designed symbols can enhance user performance, attract attention, and convey information quickly (Green & Pew, 1978; Herschler, 1999; Leonard, 2000; McDougall, deBruijn, & Curry, 2000; Wolff & Wogalter, 1998; Young & Wogalter, 2000). In general, users can recognize well-constructed symbols more rapidly and accurately than written words and using well-designed symbols can reduce time and confusion when dealing with alternative systems, control devices, and displays (Green & Pew).

Using visual symbols to convey information is not always advantageous, however. Too many symbols on a particular display or in a work area can burden user memory and cause confusion.

Often symbols are not a viable option due to equipment limitations such as minimal display space or low screen resolution. Poorly designed or inappropriately used symbols can cause more harm than good (McDougall et al., 2000).

Take an integrated approach

To maximize the benefits of symbol use, it is important to take an integrated approach to the use of symbols. This approach involves not only looking at the number of symbols on a particular system, but across the systems to which a single user is exposed and including aspects of the physical environment (i.e., ambient lighting) that might impact the effectiveness of symbols.

Previous studies have shown that the number of symbols with which a user is required to interact (size of the symbol set) can affect user performance (Blackwell & Cuomo, 1991). The larger the number of symbols, the greater the demand placed on the operator memory, leading to decreased performance (Remington & Williams, 1986). Standardization is a method used to reduce the effects of a large symbol set size by reducing the total number of symbols. The International Organization for Standardization (ISO) is endeavoring to standardize symbols encountered in basic office work (ISO/IEC, 2000a, 2000b). Lessons learned from their efforts could be applied to the AF environment. Standardization can reduce the time needed by AF specialists to learn, interpret, and respond to symbols and could minimize the risk of errors (Duncanson, 1994).

Consider the target audience

It is important to take characteristics of the target user audience into consideration to ensure symbol effectiveness. These characteristics can include the amount of system training acquired by the users, past experience with interfaces and symbols, and whether they work at a fixed position in front of the display or move around (Horton, 1994). The less training that the users have, the less chance there will be for them to learn the meaning of a symbol. Therefore, the less time there is available for training, the more important it is for the symbol to be obvious in its meaning.

Past experience with particular symbols also needs to be taken into account when examining symbols. Past experience with symbols can influence the interpretation of new symbols, as users may already associate specific meanings with those symbols. Many of us who have experience with computers associate a particular function with a symbol shaped like a folder. If a system presented us with a "folder" symbol, we would have pre-existing expectations for that symbol to act as a repository for documents.

How the users interact with symbols is also important to evaluating symbol effectiveness and designing new symbols. Users that are not positioned at a fixed distance from the display are likely to need visual symbols to convey critical information at larger viewing distances. Thus, symbols for users who move around need to be large and distinct enough to be distinguishable even at increased viewing distances. Some research suggests that when users must view information from a distance, symbols are more effective than words (Kline, Ghali, & Kline, 1990). When designing or standardizing symbols, it is critical to capture this kind of information about the users and the environment in which the symbols will be presented.

Key components of a symbol

Most symbols consist of a pictorial image surrounded by a shape with a distinct border. Some also include a text label. Each of these components is critical to effective symbol design. The pictorial image should be an effective metaphor, providing an analogy from which the user can infer the behavior of the systems that will result from activating the symbol or what the object is whose status is being represented by that symbol. Using different background shapes behind a pictorial image has proven to be effective for warning and information symbols (i.e., street signs). Although shape coding is not used as frequently in the realm of computer symbols in office environments, it can be an effective method of increasing the amount of information conveyed to the user without increasing the number of overall symbols.

Coding conventions such as color and flashing are components of a symbol often used as the users interact with the symbol or the item represented by the symbol requires user attention. Coding can be a beneficial addition to the symbol, providing the user with useful information. Kopala et al. (1983) found that color acts as an enhancer in search tasks and identification tasks, particularly as symbol density increased. Hovey and Berson (1987) and Kirkpatrick, Dutra, Lyons, Osga, and Pucci (1992) also found that the addition of color significantly improved recognition performance and allowed for faster and more accurate responses. These effects are mirrored in the self-reports from participants, who favored the color-filled symbol sets and reported their situation awareness as higher when color was used.

Previous studies on visual symbols (Ahlstrom et al., 1998; Duncanson, 1994) laid the groundwork for symbol design and evaluation in the AF environment. Other research efforts have provided for a compilation of guidelines for good interface design (Ahlstrom & Longo, 2001; DOT, 1996; ISO/IEC, 2000a, 2000b; Wagner et al., 1997). This study builds on this previous work, taking a multi-pronged approach to examining AF symbols in MCCs. This study examines the environment in which the visual symbols are present, including what other symbols exist in that work area. It catalogs the symbols and coding conventions currently in use and evaluates them against human factors best practices. It identifies where commonalities exist between systems that may be exploited for the purpose of standardization. Finally, it takes a preliminary look at the user characteristics, including how the users interact with the system.

1.2 Purpose

The purpose of this study is to catalog symbols from the systems used in AF environments and to document the coding conventions currently in use. Its secondary purpose is to provide human factors information on effective symbols. This is necessary as a resource for future symbol development and testing.

2. METHOD

The research team collected examples of current symbols from interaction with subject matter experts, software documentation, and computer-based instruction manuals. They verified these symbols and obtained information on additional symbols through conducting site visits to several GMCC and AMCC field sites. The researchers compiled information on good human factors for visual symbols through a review of current research literature and published human factors standards and guidelines documents. The research team then compared the symbols against human factors best practices.

2.1 Sites Visited

A member of the research team visited four Air Route Traffic Control Center (ARTCC) Maintenance Control Centers (AMCCs) and two General Maintenance Control Centers (GMCCs) to validate information on visual symbols collected from computer-based instruction manuals, interactions with subject matter experts, and software specifications. The sites visited were the AMCC at Washington ARTCC, the GMCC in Leesburg, VA; the AMCC in New York ARTCC at Ronkonkoma, NY; the AMCC at Cleveland ARTCC in Oberlin, OH; the AMCC at Boston ARTCC in Nashua, NH; and Boston GMCC in Boston, MA. The various sites were chosen for their proximity to the WJHTC. The researcher observed how the site personnel interacted with the various systems, what symbols were used to represent information with those systems, the number and location of symbols per screen, and the aspect of the environment that could impact symbol recognition (e.g., viewing distance and ambient illumination).

At some of the sites visited, there were more than 17 systems being utilized. The researcher observed these systems as the AF specialists interacted with them. Most of the information displays for the different systems ran different software. Some of the software was made especially for the FAA, whereas, some was Commercial-Off-The-Shelf (COTS) software.

2.2 Environments in Which the Symbols are Used

The AMCC and GMCC environments were very different. GMCCs proved to be very similar to a typical office environment. The AF specialists in this environment were positioned seated in front of the computer monitors, and the lighting was similar to a typical office environment. The AMCCs, on the other hand, were dimly lit, and the specialists moved around. (Although exact luminance levels were not measured, the observed light levels were considerably lower than a normal office environment.) The number of different systems to which the specialists were exposed was much greater at the AMCCs than the GMCCs. Appendix A contains descriptions of each of the sites visited .

2.3 Systems at Visited Sites

This section provides an overview of the systems and subsystems used by AF personnel. It includes a brief description of each system; the use of symbols; and the use of color, shapes, and other coding conventions. Table 1 compares the systems monitored and controlled at the four AMCC facilities visited.

Table 1. Comparison of Software Systems/Equipment at Different AMCCs

SYSTEM TYPE	LEESBURG	NEW YORK	CLEVELAND	BOSTON
RADARS	HOCSR HOST status HOST E1	A DSR sized monitor with Oceanic incoming routes (similar to HOCSR)	HOCSR	HOCSR
		Oceanic Display And Planning System (ODAPS), oceanic data link (three systems)		
	DSR	DSR	DSR	DSR
	WARP		WARP (M&C)	WARP (M&C)
	MCI	MCI		
	RAPPI	RAPPI	RAPPI	RAPPI
	Data Acquisition System/Real Time Status Display (DAS/RSD)	DAS/RSD (displays information for only EDARC)	DAS/RSD (using two monitors)	DAS/RSD
INPUT/OUTPUT TERMINALS	DARC	DARC (I/OT)	DARC (I/OT)	DARC (I/OT)
		Host (Input/Output Terminal) hardware management console (HMC)	HID/NAS/Local Area Network (LAN)	HOST (HMC)
		Host keyboard video display terminal (KVDT) configuration (KCNF)	KCNF	HOST (KCNF)
COMMUNICATION	VSCS	VSCS	VSCS	VSCS
	VSCS training/testing and backup system (VTABS)	VTABS	VTABS	VTABS
	RCL	RCL	LDRCL	LDRCL
	Maintenance equipment position subsystem (MPES)	MPES	MPES	MPES
	LINCS			
SYSTEM MANAGEMENT	Codex network management (Motorola)	Codex	Codex and OPUS	Codex
	Event Manager	Event Manager	Event Manager	Event Manager
REMOTE MONITORING AND CONTROL	RMM	RMM	RMM	RMM
	MASS	MASS	MASS	MASS
LOCAL ENVIRONMENTAL SYSTEMS	Environment	Facility Power Status (not a display screen)	Facility power status, fire alarms, etc... (not on display screens)	Facility Power Status (not a display screen)
	RCE		ProComm PLUS (communications battery backup system software)	
PRINTERS	Two High Speed Printers (HSP)	Two HSP NAS monitors 'no operation' input output of a logical	Two HSP for DSR	Two HSP for DSR One medium speed printer for TANDEM

2.3.1 Display System Replacement

The Display System Replacement (DSR) runs an advanced interactive executive operating system to support Air Traffic Control (ATC) missions and system management. There are three main Maintenance and Control (M&C) screens associated with the DSR (see Figures 1 and 2). The M&C Host (M&C-H) provides maintenance and control capabilities for the Host computer path and can be switched to M&C Enhanced Direct Access Radar Channel (EDARC) (M&C-E) to provide M&C capabilities for EDARC. M&C Certification (M&C-C) is used to provide certification capability.

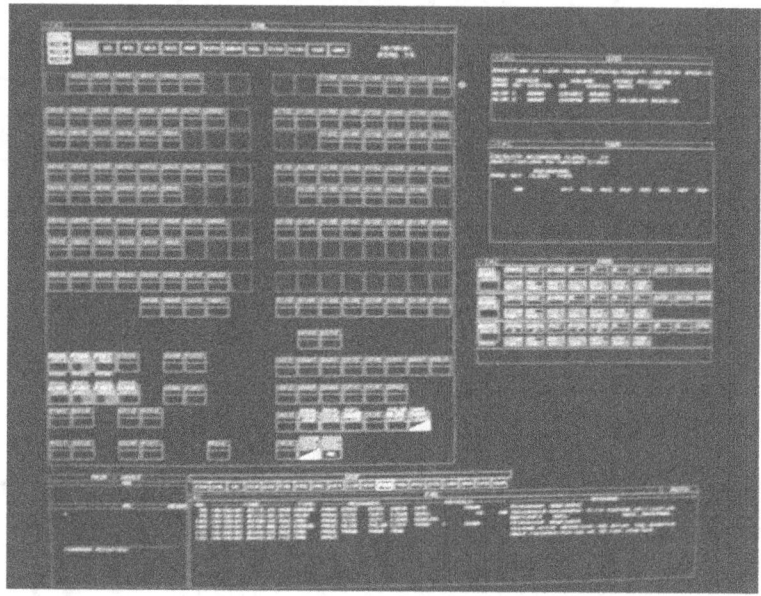

Figure 1. A primary display screen from DSR showing all three levels.

Figure 2. An alternative view of DSR showing some color coding.

DSR has three hierarchical levels on the display screen. Level 1 is a separate display area on the monitor providing columns of information representing overall system status. Level 2 is used to learn the status of specific resources (e.g., system processors, network resources, and other mid-level information). This information is also represented on a separate overlaid screen with information in columns. Level 3 is used to learn the status of specific elements within specific resources.

2.3.1.1 DSR Symbols

DSR M&C uses rectangles, triangles, or squares within a border of approximately 5/8 of an inch square. They represent radars to be monitored and controlled using a 4-letter/digit naming convention located across the top and a status box attached below.

2.3.1.2 DSR Coding

When a system goes offline due to a functional problem, it is represented by an upside down red triangle in the status box. If a corner of the status box turns yellow, this represents radar that is exhibiting degraded performance. Each symbol is outlined in green on a black background. Figure 3 presents the basic colors and symbols used for DSR monitor and control.

DSR provides two different blinking codes: on/off for status symbols and bright/dim for text. The maintenance and control uses bright/dim with white in the Facility Alert List view and the on/off blink with red and yellow in the Control Room, Processor Summary, and Local Communications Network (LCN) views. The on/off and blink rate for the symbol uses a 1 Hertz blink rate with a 50% on/off ratio. The bright/dim blink rate used for the text cycles at a 1 Hertz rate with a 75% bright/dim ratio.

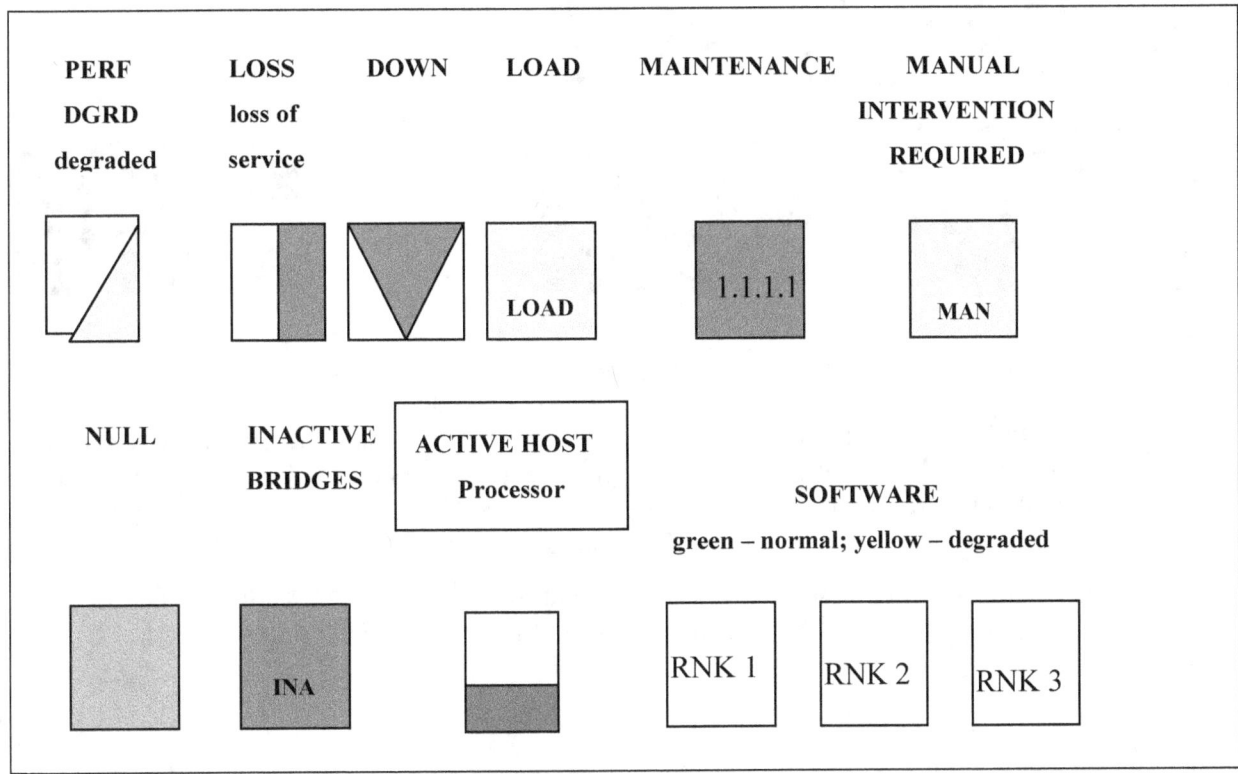

Figure 3. Basic colors and symbols coding used for DSR maintenance and control.

2.3.2 Voice Switching and Control System

The Voice Switching and Control System (VSCS) is a computer-controlled switch located at the ARTCCs, connecting the Air Traffic Controllers to pilots and other Air Traffic Controllers. It allows for the reception of air/ground (A/G) and ground/ground (G/G) communications. VSCS is a distributed switching system for intercom communications, interphone communications, Automatic Call Distribution communications, and radio communications. The VSCS M&C are located at the AMCC, and it occurs via the Maintenance Position Equipment Subsystem (MPES). The communication interface occurs via touch pad screens located at AMCCs, equipment rooms, and control floors making use of touch screens for interface with operators. At the AMCC, the touchpads are usually collocated with the DSR monitoring screens and equipment. VSCS Console Equipment (VCE) is the interface between VSCS and its operators, allowing control and access to the A/G and G/G functions. The following sections will describe the functionality of the touchpad screens and the MPES.

2.3.2.1 VSCS Symbols

VSCS symbols consist of graphic images presented in a colored rectangle, usually with an alphanumeric code. There are other rectangular boxes that contain no graphic symbols, only the alphanumeric code. Figure 4 depicts example symbols and colors seen on VSCS.

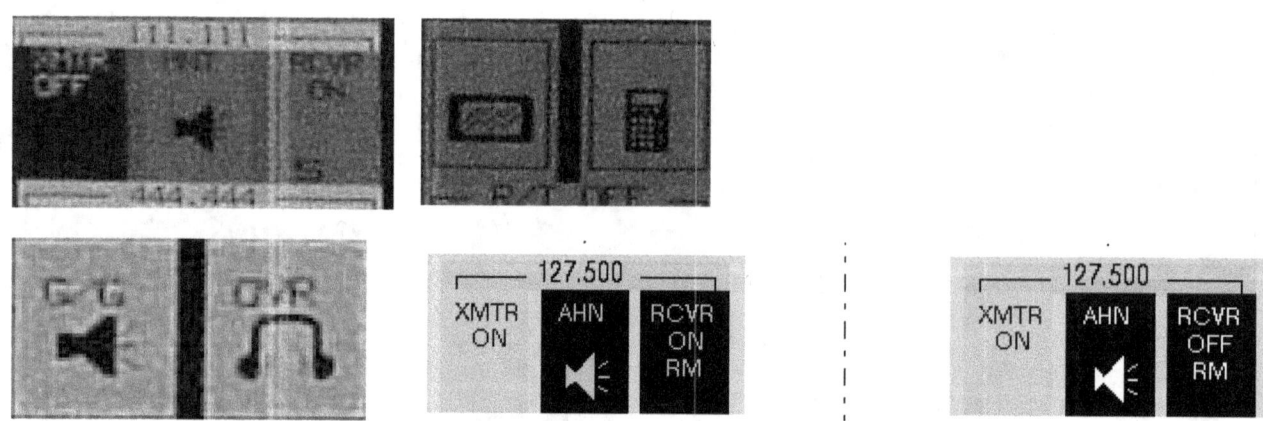

Figure 4. Example symbols seen on VSCS Touchpad.

One VSCS symbol resembles a foot pedal, and it is used to test the functionality of the foot pedal switch. Another symbol resembles a display screen, and it accesses the VSCS Display Module (VDM). A symbol that resembles a calculator is used for the VSCS Indirect Access Keypad (VIK), and a symbol that resembles a loudspeaker is used to hear A/G or G/G communications.

Another significant symbol on the touch pad is one that looks like a set of headphones. Activation of this symbol allows the operator to switch the A/G or G/G communications to particular specialist or controller headphones.

2.3.2.2 VSCS Coding Conventions

Table 2 provides color and flash coding used for VSCS.

8

Table 2. Color and Modulation Coding for VSCS Touchpad

CONDITION	BACKGROUND	TEXT	MODULATION
Unselected Frequency (A/G), Idle Direct Access call (G/G), Idle test (UTIL)	white	black	steady
Unselected Emergency Frequency (A/G)	white	red	steady
Transmitter (XMTR)/Receiver (RCVR) disabled (A/G)	black	white	steady
PTT Timeout (radio not responding) (A/G)	black	yellow	flashing
RCVR locally OFF with a squelch break (A/G)	black	amber	fluttering
RCVR remotely muted, locally ON (A/G)	black	green	steady
Backup Emergency Communications mode XMTR or RCVR OFF	black	yellow	steady
Direct Access Busy (G/G)	black	green	flashing
Screen Background (All)	dark gray	no text	N/A
Separators within frequency button groups (A/G)	medium gray	no text	N/A
Button unassigned (All)	light gray	no text	N/A
Function button assigned but currently unavailable (All)	light gray	black	steady
Available areas for second touch in two-step function (All), Classmark (on frequency indicator) (A/G), Active Progressive conference member (G/G)	violet	white	steady
Touch feedback (All)	blue	white	steady
Function available (All)	turquoise	black	steady
Active function or test (All), XMTR, RCVR, HS/LS ON (A/G), Active DA and CA calls (G/G)	green	black	steady
First step of two-step function (All)	green	black	flashing
Ringback on DA buttons (G/G)	green/white	black	flashing
Active voice monitoring (G/G)	green	white	steady
Emergency Push-To-Talk (PTT) button or frequency indicator (A/G)	red	white	steady
Active message area (All), Blocked PTT (A/G), Failed test (UTIL)	pink	black	steady
PTT confirmation (A/G)	amber	black	steady
Squelch break, RCVR ON, not RM (A/G)	amber	black	fluttering
Ringing DA/CA (G/G)	amber	black	flashing
BUEC mode XMTR and RCVR ON (A/G)	yellow	black	steady
DA/CA on hold (G/G)	yellow	black	winking

9

2.3.3 Data Acquisition Subsystem/Real-Time Status Display

Data Acquisition Subsystem/Real-Time Status Display (DAS/RSD) is made up of four display monitors depicting the current ARTCC equipment status. The displays are organized by subsystems into groups of graphical box indicators. These indicators change color to convey the status of the equipment that the boxes represent.

Table 3 presents the different subsystems that can be configured to run on the DAS/RSDs. Flashing until the change is acknowledged accompanies most status changes. Connectivity between system elements is shown as lines for some systems with color changes to indicate status. The master RSD shows all alarms for the subsystems of DAS that occupy one of the monitors. Text windows that provide cause, date, and time of problem information are accessible from the master. The master also disconnects individual data points or complete subsystems from the RSD. Depending on the ARTCC, one of the four monitors will run either Computer Display Channel (CDC) or Display Channel Complex (DCC).

Table 3. Subsystems Configured to Run on DAS/RSD

Central Control Monitoring Subsystem (CCMS)	Controls heating, ventilation, and air conditioning at the particular ARTCC; includes chillers, boilers, and air handlers.
Computer Display Channel/Display Channel Complex (CDC/DCC)	The prime radar display channels. Both systems process and display flight data update messages from the Host on the ATC's Plan View Display (PVD) and process data generated by the radar controller via the radar controls at the PVD.
Coded Time Source (CTS)	An electronic clock providing time-of-day messages to Host, Air Traffic Controllers, and High Capacity Voice Recorders (HCVR).
Environmental Control System (ECS)	Manages up to 32 fire alarms, door alarms, etc... monitored by a particular ARTCC.
Enhanced Direct Access Radar Channel (EDARC)	A backup system for the prime radar data processing channel, EDARC provides En route Air Traffic Controllers with digital radar data processing and display function if CDC/DCC is off-line.
Flight Service Data Processing System (FSDPS)	Acts as a host for up to eight Automated Flight Service Stations (AFSS). It maintains a common weather database and a separate flight database for its associated AFSS. It also monitors the status of each AFSS.
Fire Extinguishing Subsystem (HALON)	Can accommodate up to eight extinguishing system alarms from that ARTCC.
High Capacity Voice Recorders (HCVR)	Records conversations between Air Traffic Controllers and pilots to ensure adequate records. It is designed to improve controller communication techniques.
Host	The central point for the collection, processing, and distribution of data. Run on an IBM 3083BX computer and controlled by NAS operational software.
National Airspace Data Interchange Network (NADIN)	A G/G digital message-switching network. Used to exchange information on air traffic among FAA facilities and other agencies.
Non-Radar Keyboard Multiplexer	Provides the interface between the console positions and the Host for non-radar data storage and processing operations.
Power Conditioning System (PCS)	Maintains continuous power to ARTCC systems. In emergency situations it provides battery backup until generators can assume the load.
Plan View Display PVD	Provides information on the screens that present air traffic data to the controllers for a particular sector of air space.

2.3.3.1 DAS Symbols

The DAS/RSD does not use graphical symbols. Instead, color-coded boxes with text or alphanumeric codes represent monitored systems. Figures 5 a, b, c, and d depict four display views for DAS.

2.3.3.2 Coding Conventions

DAS/RSD Screen

Alarm status is indicated in the DAS/RSD master display screen (shown in Figure 5a) when a subsystem button changes to start flashing gray to red. Message information for that alarm appears in the large main text area of the page also highlighted with a flashing red color. Both the button and the information background flash at the same steady rate.

All the monitored data points can be viewed by clicking on the unmonitor (UNMON) button on the right side of the page. System monitoring is now off, and all data can be seen. If a specialist clicks on a particular item on these pages, that text changes to brown on a yellow background. Yellow is an indication that a subsystem or one of its parts is now masked. If there is only one data point in a subsystem, its corresponding button down the left side of the page will also turn yellow.

If the specialist clicks on a subsystem button in the UNMON mode, all the elements of that subsystem will appear highlighted in yellow rows with brown text. Individual subsystems can be unmasked from the UNMON mode. That system will then display alarms as if not in the UNMON mode. The subsystem button will immediately begin to flash red, and the corresponding elements that are exhibiting negative performance within that subsystem will change to white text with a red flashing background. All alarms are simultaneously presented on their respective screen and the master display screen.

The Computer Display Channel/ Display Channel Complex Screen

Figure 5b shows the CDC/DCC screen. In general, all status changes are presented with flashing, except for acknowledged alarms that have been returned to normal operating conditions. There are five major status indications on the CDC screen: MAINTENANCE and UNAVAILABLE appear as red; equipment in STANDBY mode appears as amber; equipment that is ON-LINE is green. Any indicators that appear in gray are not part of the DAS, and they are not monitored by DAS.

DAS also monitors 'performance bits' of each element, basically, subelements of the elements. If a bit becomes problematic, an indicator appears at the bottom of the overall element indicator with white text and a flashing red background. Performance degradation to the overall element is sensed and displayed with the following priorities: 1) Power Off, 2) Fault, 3) Over Temperature, and 4) Degradation. Once clicked on, this bit becomes acknowledged, and the flashing ceases. If the overall element becomes unavailable, the entire indicator flashes red.

The Enhanced Direct Access Radar Channel Screen

The Enhanced Direct Access Radar Channel (EDARC) screen shows Plan View Display (PVD) data on the lower portion of the screen. Figure 5c shows this screen. EDARC status is on top. When any PVD is going to a power-off mode, the indicator turns red and flashes. Performance display priority for the bits of these elements is: 1) Over Temperature, 2) Error, and 3) Fault. These are presented in the same way as the CDC/DCC screen. Four major states are conveyed for the elements: UNAVAILABLE appears as red, ON-LINE is green, STANDBY is amber, and gray is not monitored by DAS. Lines demonstrating connectivity with the EDARC display (buses) also change color with the same convention.

The Power Conditioning System Screen

The Power Conditioning System (PCS) screen shows the status of the PCS (shown in Figure 5d).

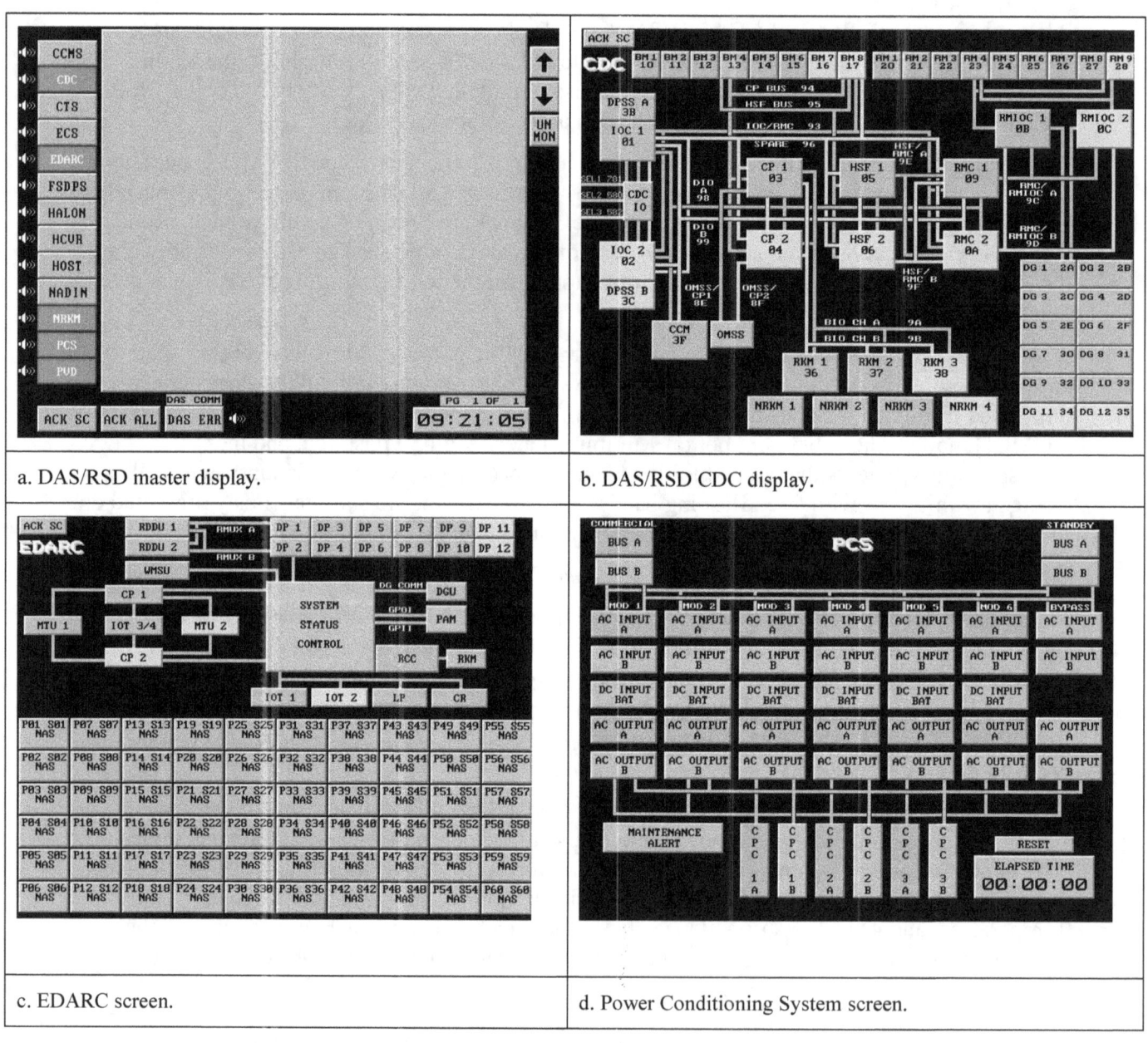

a. DAS/RSD master display.

b. DAS/RSD CDC display.

c. EDARC screen.

d. Power Conditioning System screen.

Figure 5. DAS/RSD display views.

On-line 'A' elements (except on standby or bypass) appear as green, On-line 'B' elements (except on standby or bypass) appear as blue, On-line Battery elements appear as a steady red. The Maintenance Alert Button (this screen only) flashes red during an alert mode.

Additionally, these three displays (excluding the master screen) present what are called 'Disappearing Indicators.' White text on a flashing red background on what looks like a rectangular button 'appears' when the conditions they represent are active. Once this type of alarm is acknowledged with a mouse click, it disappears from the screen.

2.3.4 Digital Voice Recording System

The Digital Voice Recording System (DVRS) provides voice-recording capability between Air Traffic Controllers, pilots, and ground Air Traffic (AT) facilities. DVRS is a COTS system, customized for the FAA. It is run on a Microsoft® Windows platform with NiceLog software. The DVRS records all voice communication involving AT activities. It reproduces, duplicates, and, after 15 days, erases recorded voice communication data. It synchronizes time of day information to Universal Coordinate Time (UCT) and records a time code synchronized with an external time source or internal Coded Time Source (CTS). DVRS provides automatic shutdown in the event of power failure, media failure, or end of media detection. It initiates an automatic switchover to a secondary Dynamic Address Translation (DAT) drive for any failure of the record function.

DVRS generates system alarms for 1) switchover to secondary DAT, 2) failure of power supply, 3) loss of time code, or 4) record malfunction. It monitors recordings and playback of single or two simultaneous channels. It interfaces with VSCS equipment, providing continuous self-test capabilities with remote alarm failure indicators. Figure 6 shows the DVRS opening page symbols and several of the NiceLog views.

2.3.4.1 DVRS Symbols

Table 4 depicts symbols associated with DVRS.

2.3.4.2 DVRS Coding Conventions

The only coding convention for DVRS is that when a particular item (e.g., channel on the page shown) is chosen from a particular screen or popup, the color of the row chosen turns blue and the text in that row turns to white (inverse highlighting).

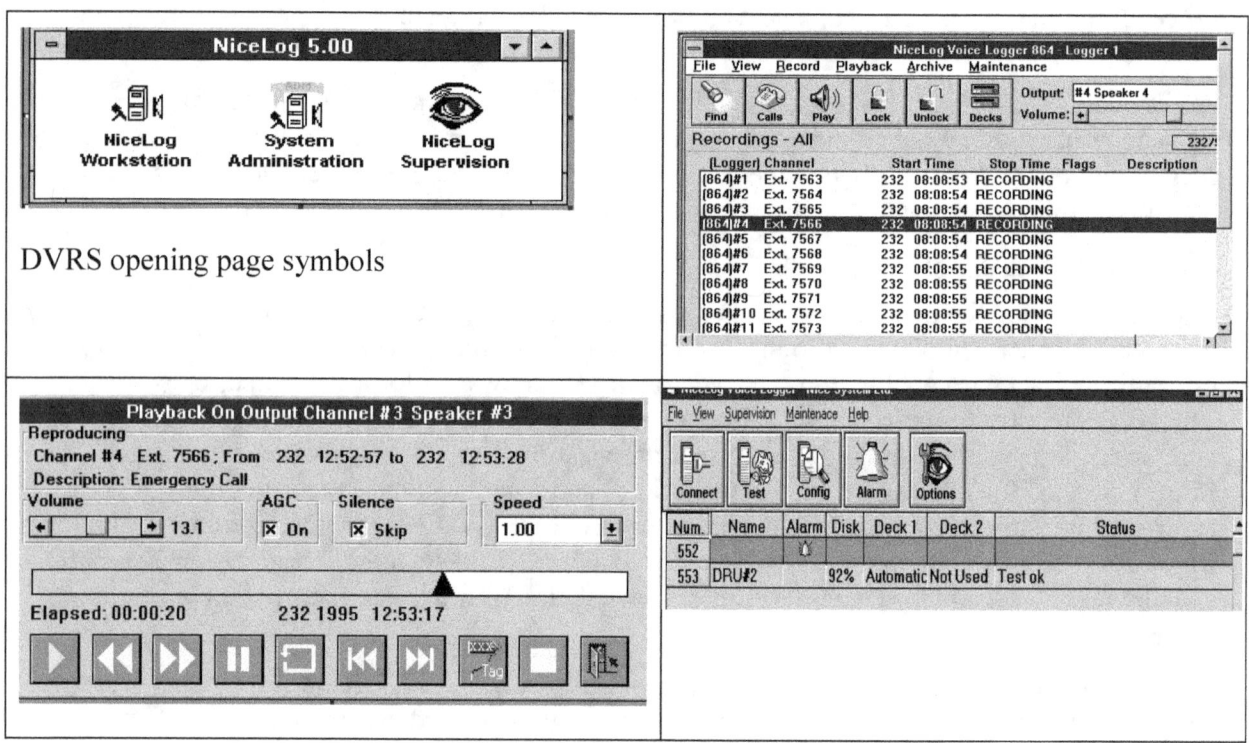

Figure 6. DVRS opening page symbols and NiceLog views.

Table 4. Symbols Associated With DVRS

Find	Allows user to locate specific audio	Calls	A list of telephone recordings	Play	Permits specific audio to be played
Lock	Keeps information from being overwritten	Unlock	Allows all audio to be overwritten	Decks	Allows user to choose different decks for archiving and retrieval
Monitor	User can monitor live audio one channel at a time	Setup	Permits User to establishes parameters for each channel	Options	Opens the supervisors options window. This allows access to the configuration of various operations parameters
Alarm	Enables/disables the Nice Log supervisors alarm for an operator selected from the supervisors window	Config	Allows the supervisor to view the configuration on a selected operators hard disk	Test	Used by the supervisor to display the results of operators most recent self-test
Connect	Allows supervisor to connect to an operator; it is a list of all DRU's/operators that can be selected		Moves tape back 10 seconds		Moves tape forward 10 seconds
	Stops audio at that point, button changes from yellow to red	Loop	Permits repetition of selected audio selections		Jumps past silence to previous active segment
	Jumps past silence to next active segment		Permits tagging of selected audio, a red tag appears above the graphical time scale		Ends recording operations
	Exits the playback mode	(((•)))	When present this symbol indicates that audio is detected		When present this symbol indicates that a channel is being recorded
	When present, this monitor symbol indicates which channel is being monitored				

2.3.5 Codex

Codex is a network management system from Motorola. It is used to monitor, test, and reconfigure communication networks at ARTCCs and TRACONs. It can manage a variety of devices simultaneously via a broad set of management applications that allow the user to configure, diagnose, and fine tune networks. It incorporates trend analyses and history event queries to resolve network faults and determine future needs.

In Codex, views may correspond to geographical locations, types of devices, network applications, or any other criterion as decided by the administrator. Symbols are graphic representations of devices or lines. These symbols make device connections and functions immediately visible.

2.3.5.1 Codex Symbols

Table 5 shows Codex symbols.

Table 5. Codex Symbols and Associated Meanings

Symbol	Meaning	Symbol	Meaning	Symbol	Meaning
	Used to draw all types of lines, and to relay connectivity information to the operator		This represents the 9820 CAP		This represents the 3600 modem
	Used to disconnect all types of lines between devices		This represents a central processing unit CPU or Service System		This Symbol represents the Event/Laser Printer
	Used to relocate a drop on a multipoint line		This represents the A/B switch		This represents a Dual Dial Restoral DDR
	Used with all types of lines to add a point where a line can bend		This is used to represent an A/B switch crossover		This symbol represents the 6250 Time Division Multiplexer TDM
	Used with all types of lines to delete a bend point		This is a representation for the 6250 Network Port Card NPC or for a Synchronous Data Card SDC		This is the only aggregate symbol available for FAA use
	Used to cancel a previously selected symbol and restore the symbol palette to its normal condition		This symbol represents the 9850 workstation base and secondary nodes		This symbol represents the 2185 Digital Bridge
	This represents a Single Line Restoral SLR				

2.3.5.2 Codex Coding Conventions

In Codex, a color change with a symbol represents a change in status. With Codex, particular system element indicators will change color to specify a down (red) or degraded (yellow) performance condition. When any subordinate device has a fault, the aggregate symbol changes color. Lines are considered as separate symbols, and they demonstrate the connectivity between

16

objects in a view. One of six different lines may be used to represent different requirements. Codex uses inverse video to highlight different options. Figure 7 shows examples of color coding for Codex screens.

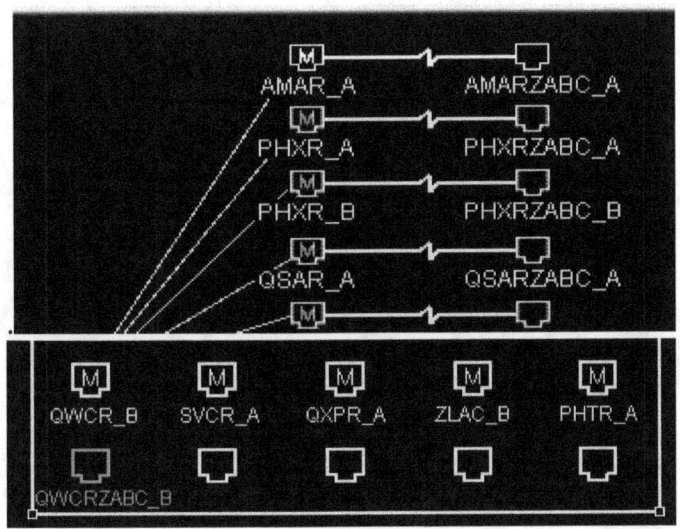

Figure 7. Examples of color coding for Codex screens.

2.3.6 Oceanic Display and Planning System

Oceanic Display and Planning System (ODAPS) exchanges flight plan data and general flight information with adjacent NAS Central Computer Complexes (CCC). Monitoring and control for ODAPS takes place at the AMCC. ODAPS information is presented on multiple 19-inch monitors. The system console located in the operator's area allows for start-up/shutdown, resets of equipment, and control of ODAPS high-speed printers. The display station monitors messages from the processors and allows the entry of text-based commands to the processors (e.g., diagnostics and configuration commands). The Keyboard Video Display Terminal (KVDT) allows for many command and control functions including control of remote alarm panels and other notifications to the NAS Area Specialist (NAS)/NAS Operations Manager (NOM). Figure 8 presents an ODAPS display screen.

2.3.6.1 ODAPS Symbols

There are no symbols for this system, only green text on a black screen. However, there are four code letters – O (operational/on-line), I (inactive/inaccessible), T (test), and R (redundant – ready to come on-line), which are used to indicate status information.

2.3.6.2 ODAPS Coding Conventions

ODAPS does not use color, flashing, or other coding conventions to indicate status information.

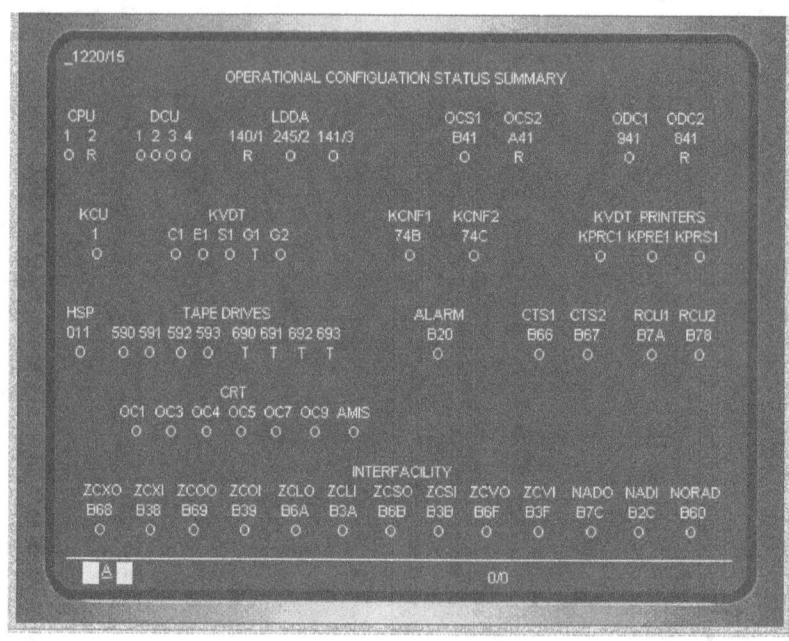

Figure 8. ODAPS – Reconfiguration and status.

2.3.7 Low Density Radio Communications Link

The Low Density Radio Communications Link (LDRCL) monitors the remote microwave systems. RCL provides interfacility transfer of digital and analog data in the NAS. It is considered a backbone system that can pass any type of data except for broadband video. It is used primarily to relay national telephone communication traffic and status/control information between Area Control Facilities (ACFs). Maintenance and control of the RCL takes place at the ARTCC by tracking and controlling the RCL microwave radio hardware.

The terminal screen of the software used to monitor this system is partitioned into three sections. The top section provides two lines of information: the upper line contains system level messages; the lower line displays the number of alarms by severity (i.e., the three levels: Critical, Major, or Minor/None are always placed in the center of the section with number of alarms preceding and updated). Figures 9 a and b show screen views. The alarm displays area (User Work Area) is the large middle area of the screen in Figure 9a. This area displays alarm reports (masks) and command line windows. The lower section of the screen is the command line area consisting of two lines. The upper line presents command syntax help and diagnostic messages. The lower line is where users can logon and enter commands. The row of selectable buttons at the bottom of the screen is also activated with the function keys on the keyboard (see Table 6).

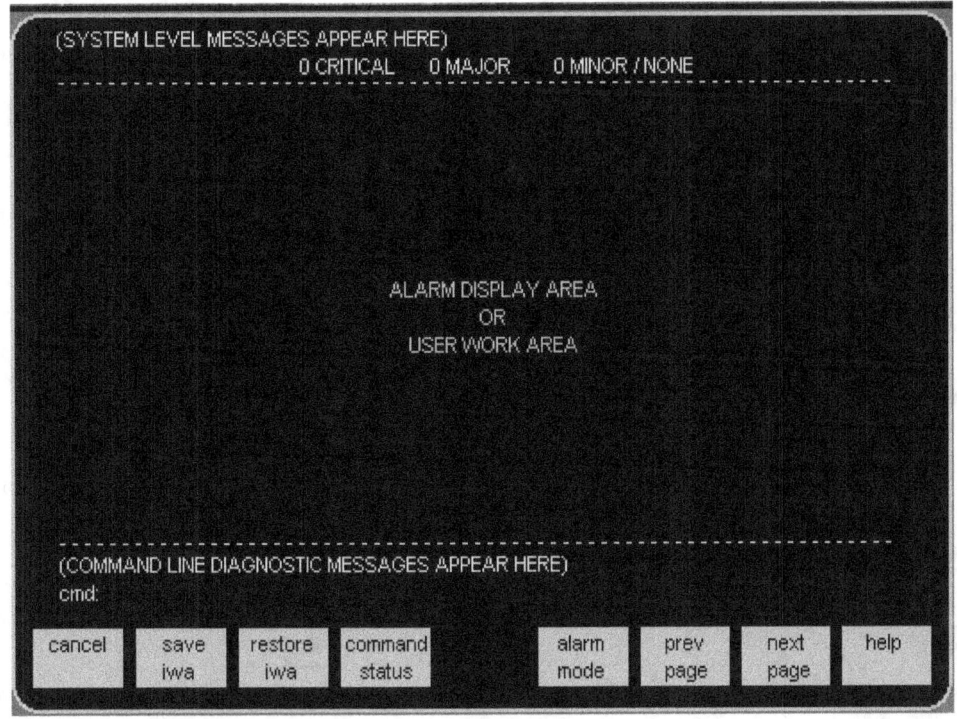

Figure 9a. Terminal screen partitions.

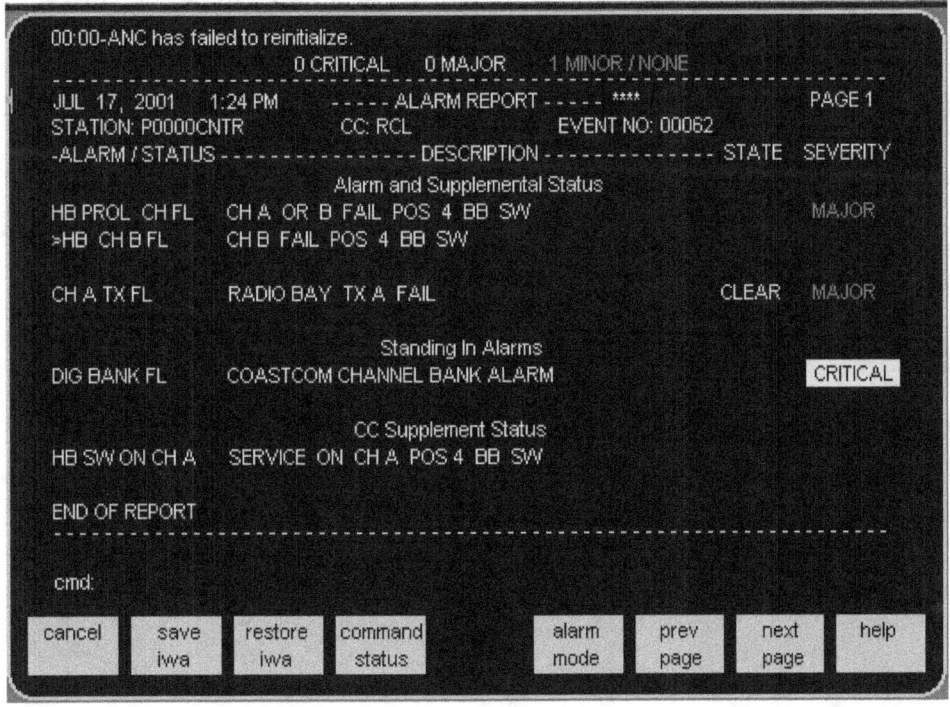

Figure 9b. Viewing and interpreting alarms.

Table 6. Buttons Always Present on the Screen

cancel	F1	Cancels a command that has been entered but not completed.
save iwa	F2	Saves information the user is working on in the Interscreen Work Area.
restore iwa	F3	Restores the information temporarily saved with the F2 function.
command status	F4	Has two purposes: user can make inquiries into the status of a command in progress (i.e., time between the command being entered but yet responded to); and when no command is being entered a command window (stack) will appear holding up to ten of the most recent commands entered.
alarm mode	F5	Returns screen to the alarm-reporting mode. The alarm mode is the default screen when no user is logged in.
prev page	F6	Views a previous screen or previous alarm report in the User Work Area.
next page	F7	Views the next screen of information or next alarm report.
help	F8	Opens 'windows' with usable text for the command line or to find data for the user work area fields.

2.3.8 Host and Oceanic Computer System Replacement

The Host and Oceanic Computer System Replacement (HOCSR) will provide operational and support storage capabilities for NAS and the support processor. The HOCSR maintenance and control provides an interface for the storage subsystem functions. Two M&C servers continually update and display the status of the subsystem. Monitor and control responsibilities include: acquiring storage subsystem configuration parameters, monitoring state and status changes, and reporting all monitored data. There are up to six HOCSR monitor and control user positions: two in the NOM area, two in the Host operations area for Computer Operators, and two in the maintenance area.

2.3.8.1 HOCSR Symbols

The initial view of HOCSR contains three symbols, one for each of the integrated cache disk arrays and one manager for everything else.

Each symbol in HOCSR uses a graphic image placed on a color-coded shape. Both the shapes and the graphic images have meanings. Figure 10 depicts the shapes used by HOCSR and their associated meanings. Table 7 presents the graphic images used for the symbols in HOCSR. Many of the images and their meanings are taken directly from a commercial program called NetView (Table 8).

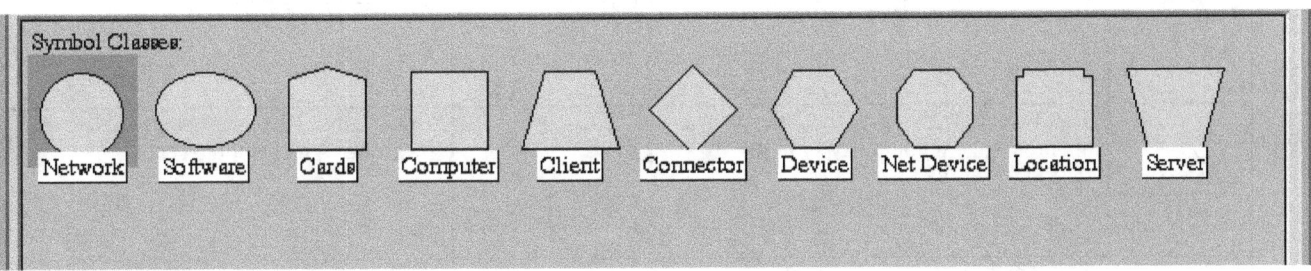

Figure 10. Background shapes used by HOCSR and their meanings.

Table 7. Symbols Used for the NetView HOCSR Interface

ICDA-1	This symbol appears on the first page of HOCSR (the root map). A double click with the mouse accesses information for the Integrated Cache Disk Array (ICDA). Two ICDA's appear on the root map.	SRVR-1	After clicking on MGR, two of these servers can be accessed from the next screen. It contains symbols for the components of a single server.
DA01bC0	This Native NetView symbol represents the systems hard drove.	HD	This symbol represents Server 1's Hard Drive status.
Dir-1	This native Net View symbol represents the system director.	ETHR-1	Two of these symbols represent Server 1's Ethernet connectivity.
Power	This Power symbol presents information on environment connectivity in the ICDA.	CTS-I/F	This symbol represents status of Server 1's Coded Time Source (CTS).
Temp	This Temperature symbol is also environmental information for the ICDA.	NMGR	This symbol represents Server 1's connectivity to the Network Manager.
MGR	The Manager (MGR) symbol allows access to all the other information pertinent to HOCSR.	EMGR	This symbol represents Server 1's access and status of the Event Manager.
AMCC1	There are multiple presentations of this symbol, which can provide access to information for AMCC 1 (shown) or 2, CO 1 or 2, or ADM 1 or 2.	SWCH-2	Two switches are also accessible from the MGR.
8-CO2	Clicking on the switch icon accesses a screen full of these symbols. These are the ports that have been configured for use with the system. Acronyms below each Port representation provide information for two 'spare' ports, ICDA's, servers, AMCC's, ADM, CO 1 and 2 (shown), and the two trunk connections between the switches themselves. There is also a Power symbol found on this screen.	PRT-1	Printer status can also be provided from the MGR symbol.

Table 8. Graphic Images Used With NetView Software

Map	Name	Image	Map	Name	Image
Root	ICDA		SRVR	HD	
	MGR			Ethr	
ICDA	Dir			CTS-I/F	
	Drive			NETWK-MGR	
	Temp			EVENT-MGR	
	Power			CTS	
MGR	Server			Temp	
	Switch			Power	
	Workstation		SWCH	Port	
	Printer			Power	

2.3.8.2 HOCSR Coding Conventions

The monitored system states are represented with color coding of the shape behind the graphic image. Green is used for normal, yellow for degraded, and red for failed. A normal green state indicates that the system is functioning normally with no reported errors. Before the color of a symbol is changed from yellow or red to green, all of the subordinate devices must be operating normally. As long as at least one subordinate symbol is yellow or red, the symbol will remain yellow. If the symbol is subordinate with no subordinate symbols of its own, then all of its previously reported warning and/or critical events must recover before the symbol is changed to green. The absence of a graphic image and the gray color of an item indicate items that are not configured for use.

A summary list of events also uses color coding. The text is black, and the background is normally gray when there are no events requiring acknowledgment. Events are represented with red, yellow, and green. Unacknowledged critical events that require immediate action because they impact NAS operations are red flashing with gray. Unacknowledged warnings appear yellow flashing with gray and require attention, but not immediately. Black text on a white background represents information messages; green represents a normal operating state.

Items that have been selected for a subsequent action (e.g., acknowledging a critical entry) for displaying detailed information about an entry or for printing the entry have selection emphasis. Red text on black background represents critical events, when selected. Yellow text on a black background represents warning events, when selected. Green text on a black background represents recovery events with selection emphasis. Finally, white text on a light-gray background represents information with selection emphasis.

A right-pointing arrow is displayed to the left of the unacknowledged entries for unacknowledged critical and warning entries. When the entry has been acknowledged, the arrow is removed for that entry. The flashing summary list header continues to flash until all critical and warning entries are acknowledged. Flash rates used for this system have not yet been determined.

Color is also used to indicate whether an auditory alarm will sound. The header of the events list is a rectangle. If the alarm is on, the rectangle will appear gray with black text saying "Alarm On." If the alarm is filtered, the background of the rectangle will appear tan, and if the alarm is off, the background of the rectangle will appear yellow (see Figure 11).

24

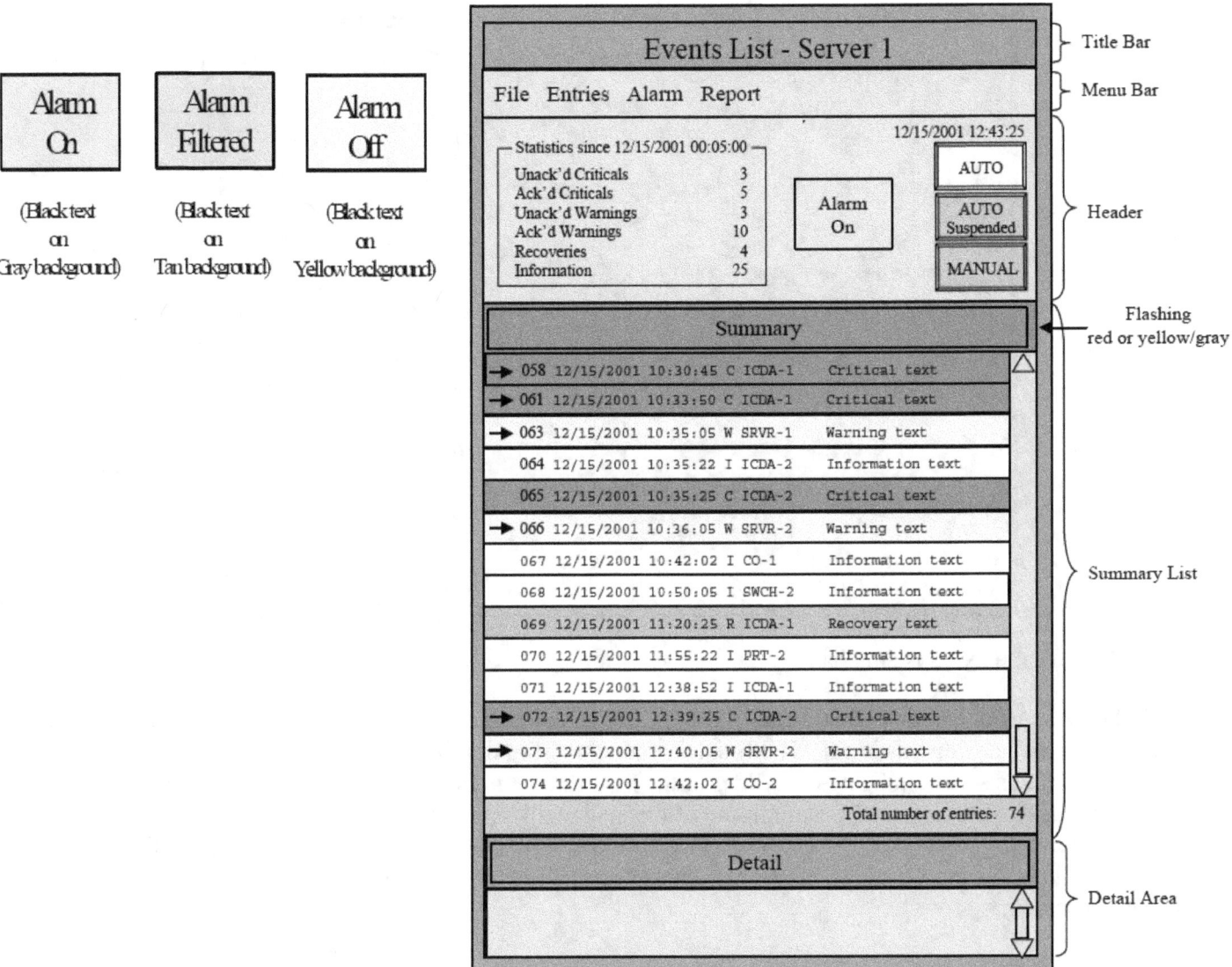

Figure 11. Color coding of HOCSR list information.

2.3.9 Host Interface Device/National Airspace System/Local Area Network

Host Interface Device/National Airspace System/Local Area Network (HNL) is an interface between ATC systems and the Central Computer Complex Host. The HNL provides communication protocol services for interfacing ATC applications with the HCS. This software is used to monitor and manage the hardware and software applications of the HNL. HNL presents information with the same NetView software as used with HOCSR.

The main page after logging on to this software program is called Segment 1. The main frame of the Segment 1 screen contains a map for the network (see Figure 12a). Each symbol on the ring represents a component of the HNL. Each symbol can be used to access ports/connections for the individual components.

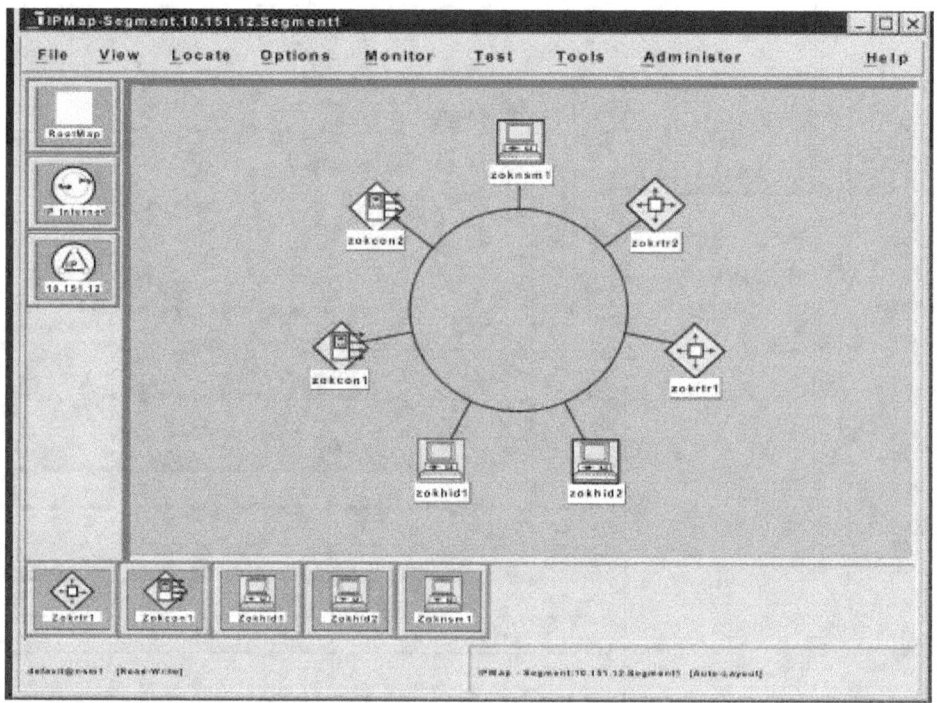

Figure 12a. HNL systems page.

The symbols at the bottom of the screen indicate the components that previously have been investigated during this login. The first three letters of the title beneath each symbol in the main frame on this screen indicate the ARTCC; the next three letters indicate the equipment type. Selecting a symbol from the main frame of this page will bring the specialist to a sub map for that particular object (see Figure 12b). The symbols on the left of the screen show the depth of access into this map system. Specialists can select the Segment 1 symbol here and return to the main screen.

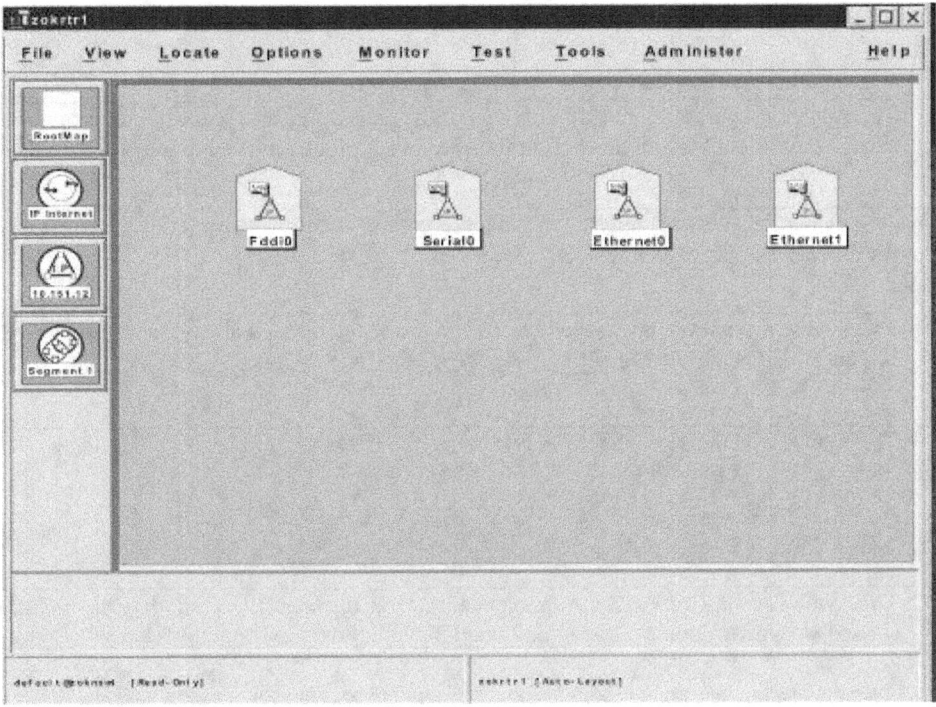

Figure 12b. HNL submap.

2.3.9.1 HNL Symbols

The HNL is run on the same NetView software as HOCSR, therefore many of the symbols are the same. As with HOCSR, the HNL has graphic images presented on a color-coded shape background. The background shapes are used to code certain items. The shape coding is the same as is used for HOCSR (see Table 9).

2.3.9.2 HNL Coding Conventions

For the HNL, the green indicates normal status. Yellow indicates marginal status, that is, the system is still operational but not normal. Red codes critical status, that is, the system is not functioning. Blue codes an unknown status. Wheat indicates that the particular object is not being managed. The color is not on the symbol itself but on the shape behind the symbol. Yellow symbols in the left column represent the current level.

Table 9. Symbols and Meanings for the HNL

SYMBOL	MEANING
	This NetView symbol, in the left columns of the pages, acts as a place holder/reminder to the specialist. By clicking on this button the specialist will be returned to the NetView set up page.
	This symbol also always appears in the left column. By clicking on it the specialist is returned to the NetView log in screen.
	By clicking on this symbol in the left column the specialist will always be returned to the Segment 1 screen, which is the Topology Map.
	This symbol, on the Topology Map represents the HIDs that are connected to the HNL.
	This symbol, in the left column of the page, informs the specialists that they have reached the second level after double clicking on the HID symbol on the Topology Map.
	This represents the status of the MCCA1 – an IBM protocol card, showing the status of the communication between the HID and the HOST. This is the second HID screen.
	Also the second screen of HID. Access and status to the HID software connections.
	These symbols appear on the third page of information for the HID processes, when the symbol immediately above is double clicked. They are status and access to the interface designations. Transport and Network (TRN), Maintenance and Diagnostics (MNT – shown), and Channel Interface (CHN).
	This is a representation of the routers connected to this HNL.
	This is the representation for the Fiber Distributed Data Interface (FDDI) connection on the second and final page accessible after double clicking on Router 1.
	If Router 2 is double clicked from the topology map this symbol appears. It is used to represent the FDDI connection, the connection to the E-Com screen (shown), and connection to the Center TRACONs Automation System (CTAS). This symbol also is used to represent Ethernet and some serial port connectivity.
	This symbol appears on the same screen as immediately above. It is also the representation of serial port connectivity. In this instance an 'Unmanaged' serial port connection.

Table 9. Symbols and Meanings for the HNL (Cont.)

SYMBOL	MEANING
	This is a representation of the concentrators connected to this HNL.
	This is the meaning for the FDDI on the second screen available for concentrators.
	This symbol on the concentrator sub map reflects status of and allows access to the various Ports accessible via concentrators.
	After clicking on the ports symbol (immediately above) the specialist comes to the final page of concentrators. This particular port connection shows the status of connectivity to Router 1.
	This is the representation for the lone Network System Manager connected to this HNL.
	This represents the FDDI connection to the network. The second screen available after double clicking on the Network System Manager from the Segment 1 – topology map screen.

2.3.10 Interim Maintenance Console System

The IMCS allows remote monitoring and control of facilities so that equipment performance monitoring, control, and certification can occur from a centralized work center. Using Outside View software, an AF specialist can retrieve an open log to document alarms and status changes. Information includes the date and time of acknowledgement. Additional screens provide status information for the various subsystems monitored by the IMCS and a site directory screen.

The IMCS is comprised of eight navigation screens: the constant monitor screen with functions menu, acknowledged alarms, an active alarms screen, a full site directory, a partition status screen, the site status screen, a commands screen, and the M&C software menu screen. Some of these navigation screens are shown in Figure 13a, b, c, and d. The screen that is shown most of the time is the site status screen, from which the specialist can acknowledge alarms and warnings, open a manual entry screen, or go to the command screen.

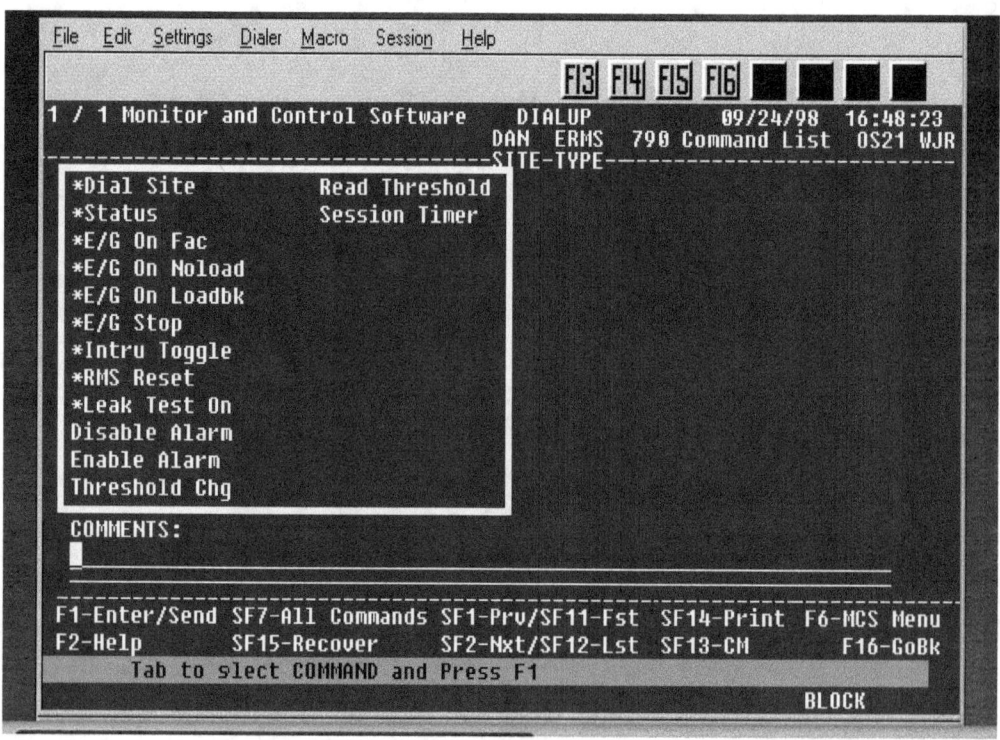

Figure 13a. IMCS Command List Screen (available commands highlighted in yellow).

```
 1 /  2 Monitor and Control Software DIRECT        12/18/98  15:38:45
    STATUS                      SAN  ERMS          Site Status  OS21 WJR
---------------------------------SITE-TYPE----------------------------------
CNTRL F LUID POINT DESCRIPTION     POINT VALUE        ENTRY DATE/TIME
   M     0099 MPS/RMS Comm. ALERT   DISCONNECTED      12/18/98 15:38:42
   M     2001 Last Cmd Recvd        Status            12/18/98 15:26:22
   M     2002 Last Cmd Result       Executed          12/18/98 15:26:23
   M     2003 Local/Remote          Remote            12/18/98 15:26:21
   M     2004 Local User                              12/18/98 15:26:21
   M     2007 EQ Analog Unit 1      Comm Normal       12/18/98 15:26:21
   M     2008 EQ Digital Unit 1     Comm Normal       12/18/98 15:26:22
   M     2009 RMS Backup Battery    Normal            12/18/98 15:26:22
   M     200A RMS Temperature              102.2      12/18/98 15:26:22
   M     200B RMS Voltage                  107.4      12/18/98 15:26:22
   M     2201 Fire System           Normal            12/18/98 15:26:25
   M     2202 Fuel System Comm      Normal            12/18/98 15:26:25
   M     2203 Tank 1 Volume (gal)          100        12/18/98 15:35:11
   M     2204 Tank 1 Water Lvl(in)          0.0       12/18/98 15:26:25
   M     2205 Tank 1 Leak Test      Pass              12/18/98 15:37:35
   M     2206 Leak Detector         Normal            12/18/98 15:26:26
F1-SiteStat F4-AlarmLst F7-Command SF1-Prv/SF11-Fst SF8-NR/MES F6-MCS Menu
F3-SiteInfo F5-AlarmAck F8-Control SF2-Nxt/SF12-Lst SF15-Recov F16-GoBk
              Tab to the Alarm to be acknowledged and Press F5
```

Figure 13b. IMCS Site Status Screen.

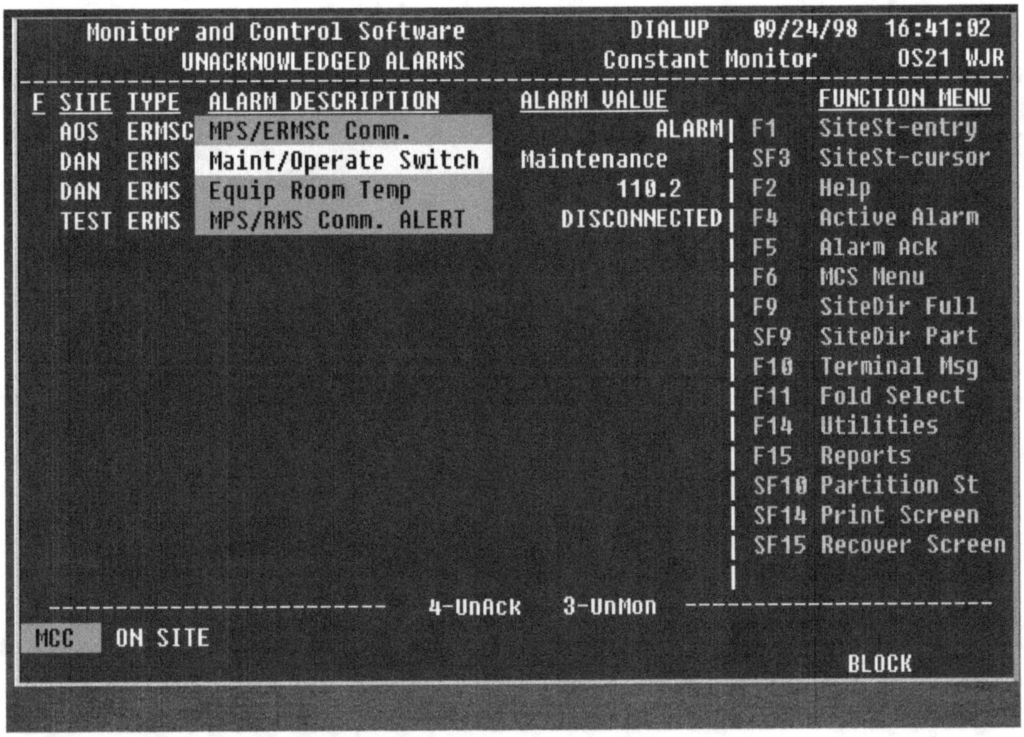

Figure 13c. IMCS Constant Monitor Screen.

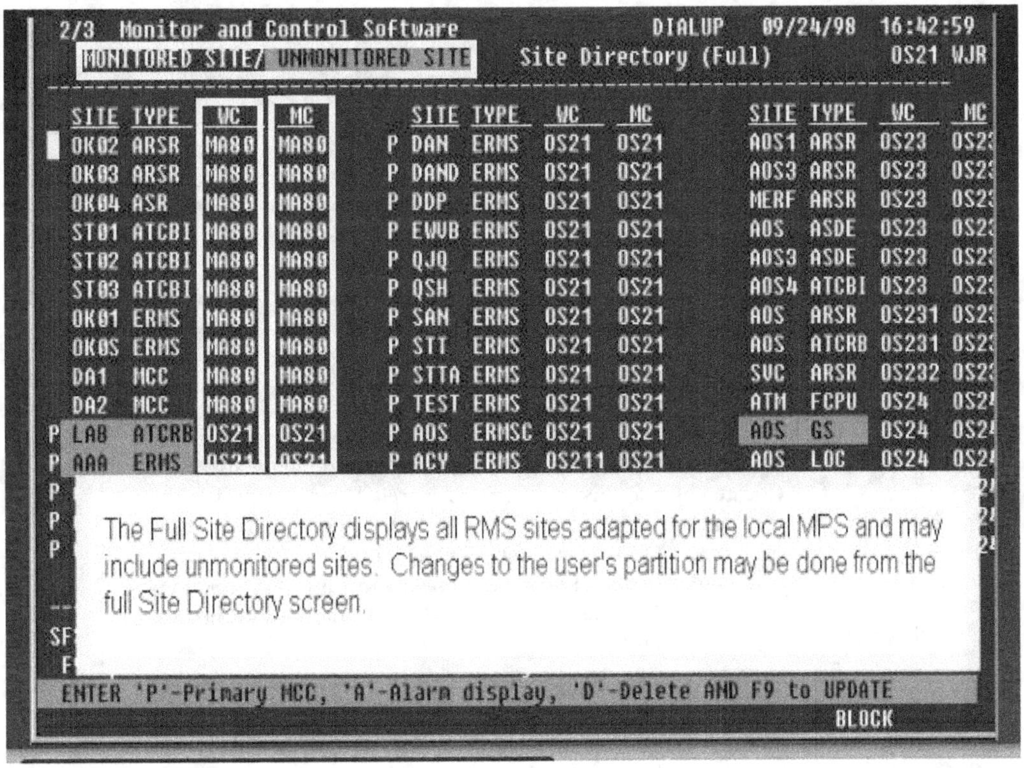

Figure 13d. IMCS Site Directory Screen.

2.3.10.1 IMCS Symbols

The majority of the IMCS program is text-based, with only a few symbols present across the top of the IMCS screens. Table 10 depicts these symbols.

Table 10. Symbols that Appear Across the Top of the IMCS/MMS Screens

	This is the Outside View software "Print On" command.
	This symbol represents the "COPY" command for the Tandem emulator.
	This represents the outside view "PASTE" command.
	This symbol permits access to the emulation phone book.
	This permits the specialist the opportunity to "hang up" a circuit.
	Allows the specialist reconnection to the last session.
	This provides the specialist the capability to customize the screens colors.
	This symbol allows the specialist to change the font style.
	This symbol and a like one with a downward facing arrow (located next to this one) are considered "Transfer Utilities" these are used by the Tandem system to "initiate" file transfers, or "retrieve" (downward facing yellow arrow) files into a personal computer (PC) format for manipulations on specialists personal PC's. The letters IXF represent the term Information Xchange Facility.

2.3.10.2 IMCS Coding Conventions

In the IMCS, information is usually in white text on the blue screen. When red highlights a row of information, it designates an alarm status (e.g., system is down or failed and action needs to be taken). When yellow highlights a row of information, it designates an alert status (e.g., a system or part of a system is on the verge of failure).

2.3.11 Maintenance Monitoring System

The MMS is set up with Tandem in order to provide more direct interaction with the Event Manager system. It is very similar to IMCS in appearance, relying on the same Outside View software interface.

2.3.11.1 MMS Symbols

The symbols for the MMS are the same as those shown for IMCS. Besides these symbols, much data are linked from this system to the Tandem via pop-up windows. Additionally, while interacting with the system, specialists must enter a wide range of precise commands onto specific 'lines' in the main content areas of the display pages and into the pop-up windows.

2.3.11.2 MMS Coding Conventions

With both the IMCS and MMS, information is usually in white text on the blue screen. With MMS, some text is highlighted with a gray background, and the text appears as the same blue color as the main area of the screen. A yellow rectangular cursor indicates the next line where information needs to be entered.

A status/information bar is located at the bottom of the main display pages. When the bar is red with blue text, it indicates that a Macro is being enabled. Macros are previously written instructions for the Tandem system. When the bar is white with blue text, it is either informing the specialist that some activity is taking place within Tandem, or the system is requesting that the specialist take some specific action.

2.3.12 Maintenance Automation System Software

The MASS is a replacement for the IMCS. MASS is designed to perform real-time monitoring of NAS facilities and subsystems that are part of the FAA RMMS, remotely control subsystems in the RMMS, remotely control subsystem states, and perform system diagnostics.

ERMS is an example of one of the many subsystems that feed data to MASS. The ERMS monitors the environmental data at FAA facilities. The data accumulated by the ERMS include information on processor temperatures, fire alarm status, fuel levels, and facility security. This information is passed via MASS to AF specialists.

MASS functions in a windows environment, with basic windows components including: title bar, menu bar, window bar, the operator bar, and a status bar. The minimized MASS symbol is an abbreviated version of the status bar.

The primary window used in MASS is the System Monitor. The System Monitor displays the subsystem information. It has three different views: 1) the Alarm List View displays data for subsystems in the current profile that have alarms, alerts, and other operational status indicators; 2) the Site List View lists all the subsystems in the current profile, providing an indication of the operational status of each subsystem; and 3) the Unacknowledged List View shows only unacknowledged alarms and alerts on the subsystems in the current profile. Figures 14a and b depict the Alarm List View. Other possible views are the Quick Look View and the Unacknowledged List View, depicted in Figures 14c and d.

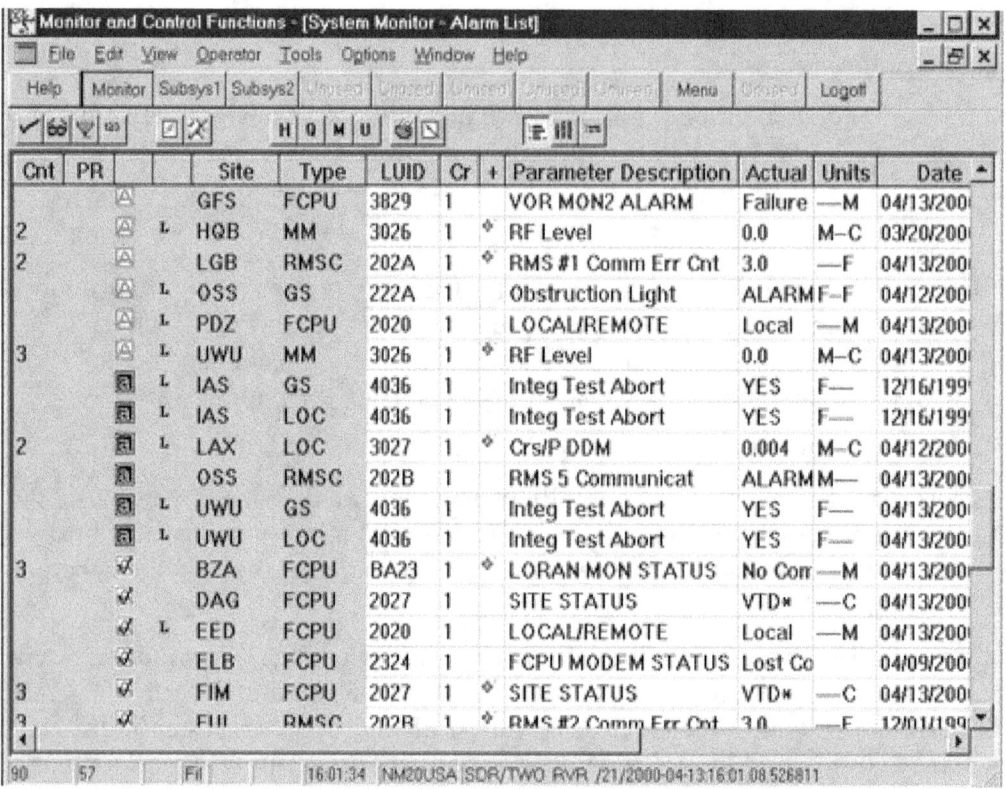

Cnt	PR			Site	Type	LUID	Cr	+	Parameter Description	Actual	Units	Date
				GFS	FCPU	3829	1		VOR MON2 ALARM	Failure	—M	04/13/200(
2		L		HQB	MM	3026	1	◊	RF Level	0.0	M–C	03/20/200(
2				LGB	RMSC	202A	1	◊	RMS #1 Comm Err Cnt	3.0	—F	04/13/200(
		L		OSS	GS	222A	1		Obstruction Light	ALARM	F–F	04/12/200(
		L		PDZ	FCPU	2020	1		LOCAL/REMOTE	Local	—M	04/13/200(
3		L		UWU	MM	3026	1	◊	RF Level	0.0	M–C	04/13/200(
		L		IAS	GS	4036	1		Integ Test Abort	YES	F—	12/16/199(
		L		IAS	LOC	4036	1		Integ Test Abort	YES	F—	12/16/199(
2		L		LAX	LOC	3027	1	◊	Crs/P DDM	0.004	M–C	04/12/200(
				OSS	RMSC	202B	1		RMS 5 Communicat	ALARM	M—	04/13/200(
		L		UWU	GS	4036	1		Integ Test Abort	YES	F—	04/13/200(
		L		UWU	LOC	4036	1		Integ Test Abort	YES	F—	04/13/200(
3				BZA	FCPU	BA23	1	◊	LORAN MON STATUS	No Con	—M	04/13/200(
				DAG	FCPU	2027	1		SITE STATUS	VTD*	—C	04/13/200(
		L		EED	FCPU	2020	1		LOCAL/REMOTE	Local	—M	04/13/200(
				ELB	FCPU	2324	1		FCPU MODEM STATUS	Lost Co		04/09/200(
3				FIM	FCPU	2027	1	◊	SITE STATUS	VTD*	—C	04/13/200(
3				FUJ	RMSC	202B	1	◊	RMS #2 Comm Err Cnt	3.0	—F	12/01/199(

Figure 14a. MASS alarm list view.

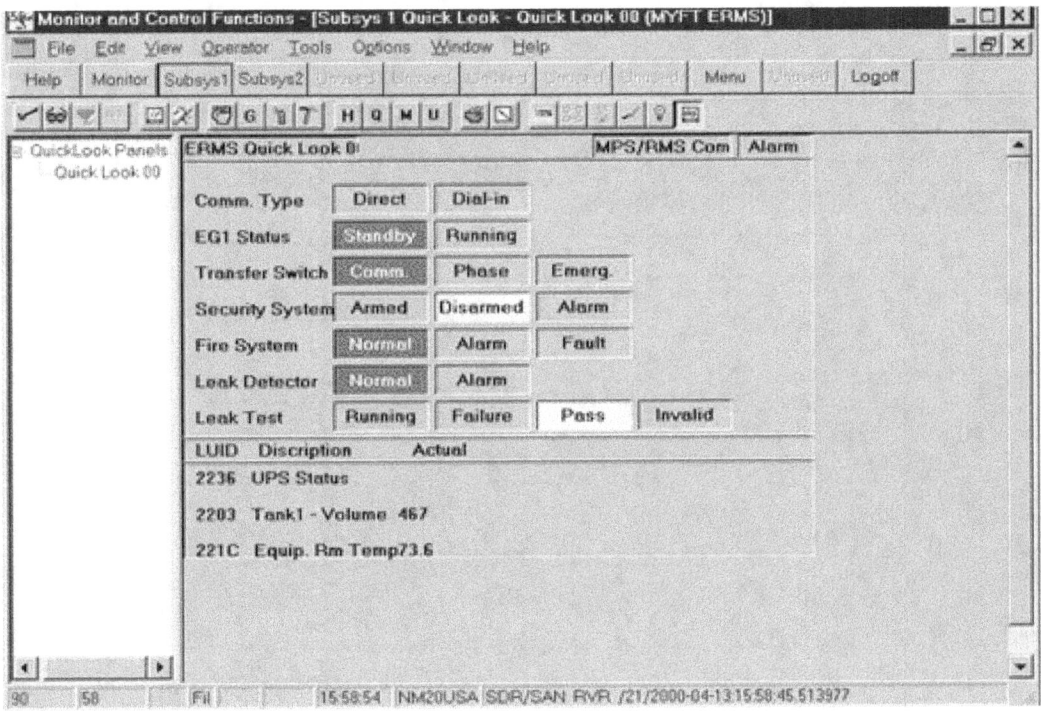

Cnt	PR			Site	Type	LUID	Cr	+	Parameter Description	Actual	Units	Date
				BLHR	ERMS	2205	1		Tank 1 Leak Test	Pass		04/09/200
5		L		GPE	GS	3036	1	✧	RF Channel	ALARM M—		04/12/200
		L		GPE	RMSC	2027	1		RMS 1 Communicat	ALARM M—		04/10/200
				IWAV	ERMS	221D	1		Security System	Disarm F-C		04/13/200
				L12	ERMS	2205	1		Tank 1 Leak Test	Pass	F-C	04/09/200
		L		LAX	RMSC	202A	1		RMS 4 Communicat	ALARM M—		04/12/200
				LGBA	ERMS	2205	1		Tank 1 Leak Test	Pass	F-C	04/09/200
				LGBT	ERMS	2205	1		Tank 1 Leak Test	Pass	F-C	04/09/200
2				MYFT	ERMS	2205	1	✧	Tank 1 Leak Test	Pass	F-C	04/09/200
				NFG	ERMS	2205	1		Tank 1 Leak Test	Pass	F-C	04/07/200
				NKXA	ERMS	2205	1		Tank 1 Leak Test	Pass	F-C	04/10/200
2		L		NSD	ARSR	4827	1	✧	KIR-1B LOCKOUT LIGH Soft ala			04/13/200
6				NSD	ATCRB	2023	1	✧	Sign Out Status	Switch F—		02/23/200

Figure 14b. MASS alarm list view with ERMS information highlighted.

Figure 14c. MASS quick look view of ERMS.

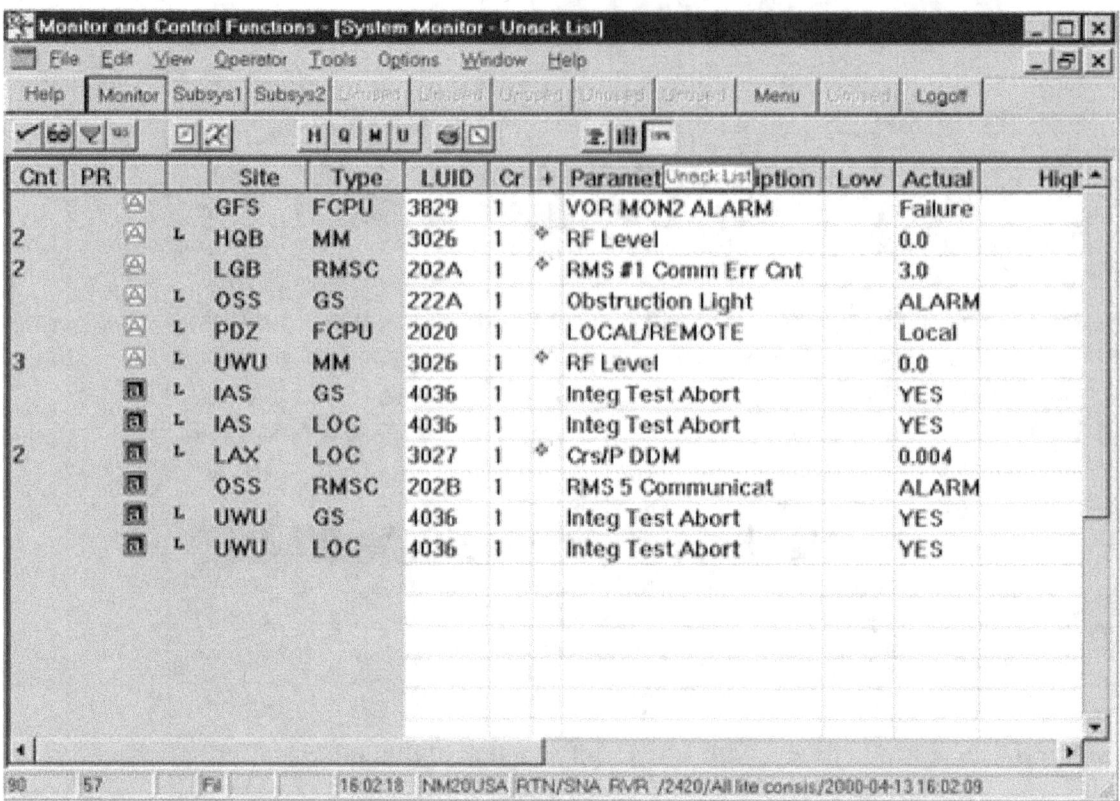

Figure 14d. MASS unacknowledged list view.

2.3.12.1 MASS Symbols

Table 11 displays the symbols used for MASS/MCF buttons. Figure 15 displays symbols and color-codes used to signify alarm and alert status.

Table 11. MASS/MCF Buttons

Button	Name	Windows	Function
✓	Acknowledge	System Monitor and Subsystem	To indicate that an Alarm or Alert has been noted
👓	Mask	System Monitor and Subsystem	To inhibit the display of alarms and alerts, for selected Data Points, on the System Monitor and Subsystem Alarm Summary display of every MDT in MASS/MCF.
▽	Filter	System Monitor and Subsystem: Alarm Summary View	To prevent specific types of subsystem status data from being displayed on an MDT.
123	Sort	System Monitor and Subsystem: Alarm Summary View	To control the order in which data on a display are listed.
✊	Assume - -	Subsystem	Assume: To assume command control of a subsystem, thereby preventing other users from sending commands to the subsystem.
✋	Relinquish	Subsystem	Relinquish: To relinquish command control of a subsystem.

Button	Name	Windows	Function
👆	Request/Take	Subsystem	Request/Take: To request assumption of control/ to take control by a user having proper authority
⚡	Commands	System Monitor and Subsystem	To send commands to a subsystem.
✗	MCF Settings	System Monitor and Subsystem	To enter (for display purposes) condition status indicators for subsystems not connected to an RMS and for conditions not monitored for subsystems connected to an RMS.
7	Pick	Subsystem	To select a subsystem which is the object of an MASS/MCF function
G	Get	Subsystem	To request a site data report from a subsystem's RMS.
⬆	Refresh	Subsystem	To update the Subsystem views with data from the MPS.

Table 11. MASS/MCF Buttons (Con't.)

Button	Name	Windows	Function
Q	Quick Desktop Settings	System Monitor and Subsystem	To provide an alternate means of controlling the type of data to be displayed and enabling certain display functions
M	System Messages	System Monitor and Subsystem	To display messages received by the MDT from the MPS.
U	UserId Lookup	System Monitor and Subsystem	To look up information about users based on the users' Ids
(printer icon)	Print Current Window	System Monitor and Subsystem	To print the data displayed in the active window.
(terminal icon)	Terminal Messages	System Monitor and Subsystem	To send and review text messages to the MPS using a bulletin board approach
H	User History	System Monitor and Subsystem	To view a list of user actions for a subsystems

2.3.12.2 MASS Coding Conventions

MASS uses red to indicate alarm status, yellow to indicate alert, blue to indicate a system state change, and green to indicate a return to normal status (see Figure 15).

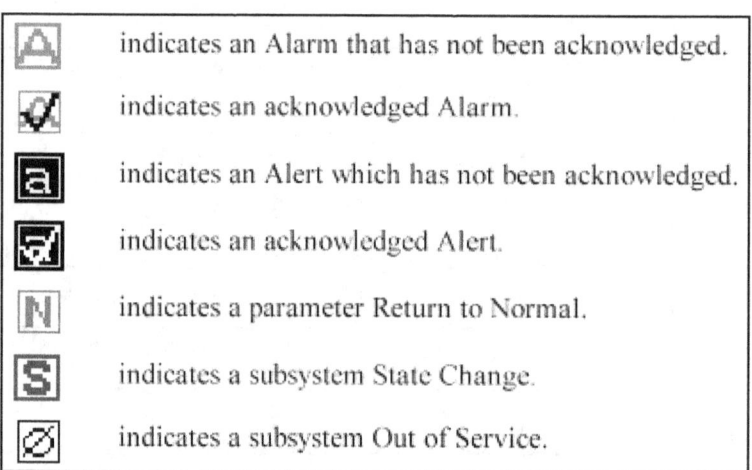

Figure 15. Symbols and color-codes used to indicate alarm and alert status in MASS.

2.3.13 Event Manager

Event Manager is designed to manage, track, and coordinate all events encountered in the day-to-day operation of a GMCC, AMCC, Service Operations Center, or Operations Control Center. These events consist of facility or service interruptions, flight check coordination, facility commissioning/decommissioning, maintenance activities not requiring an interruption, maintenance of non-FAA facilities, tracking of telephone company line problems, and problems with commercial power. The Event Manager is linked to the MMS and requires a logon using the specialist's MMS logon. This feature allows automatic population of MMS entries from the Event Manager. There are six views available for Event Manager: events display, interruption entry form, event coordination form, coordination info, facility info, and phone book sheet. These views are shown in Figure 16a. The view can be changed by selecting a different tab from across the top of the program, as shown in Figure 16b, c, d, e, and f.

Figure 16a. Event Manager events display.

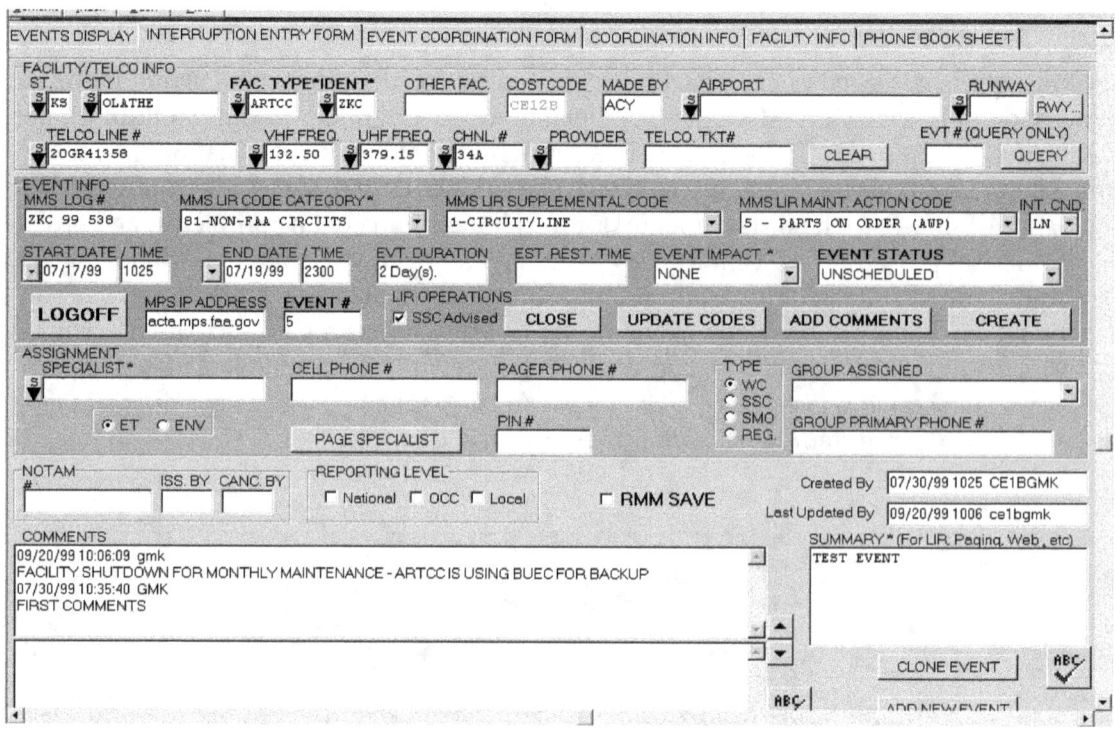

Figure 16b. Event Manager interruption entry form.

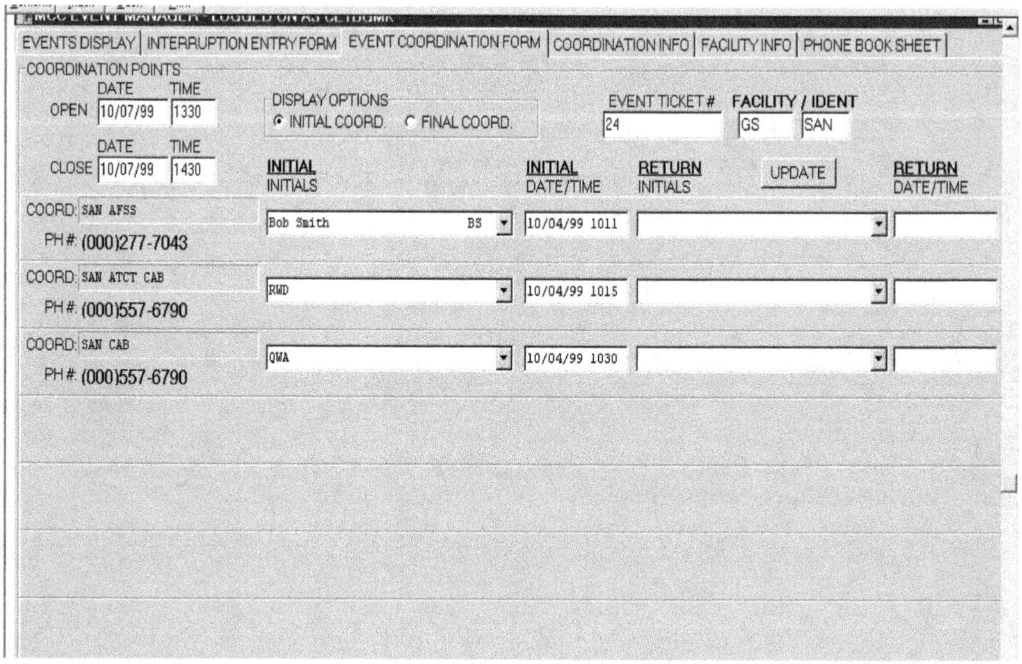

Figure 16c. Event Manager event coordination form.

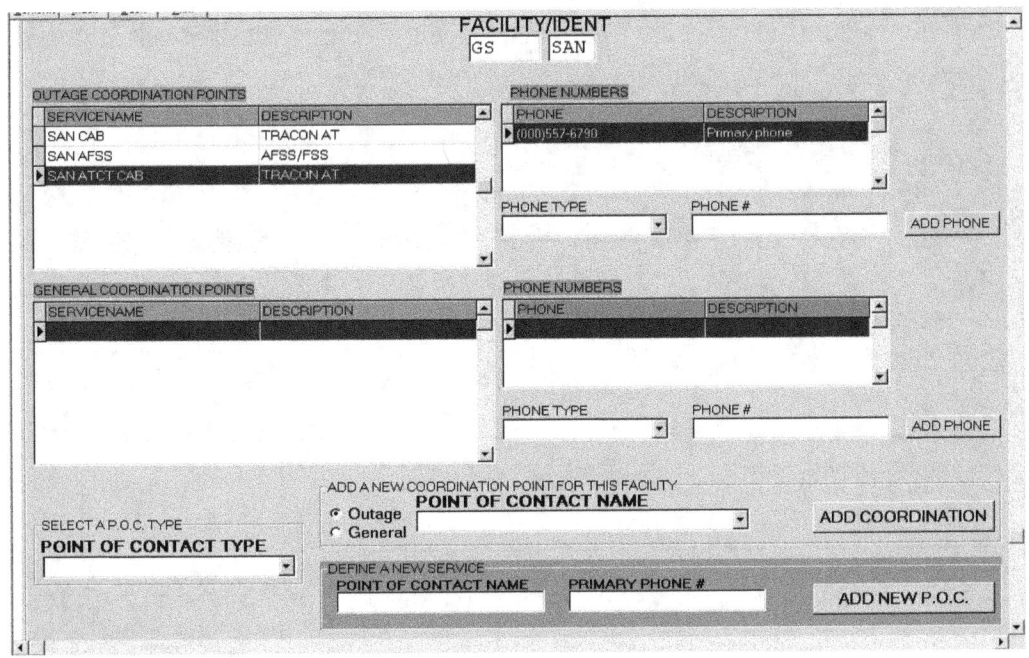

Figure 16d. Event Manager coordination information form.

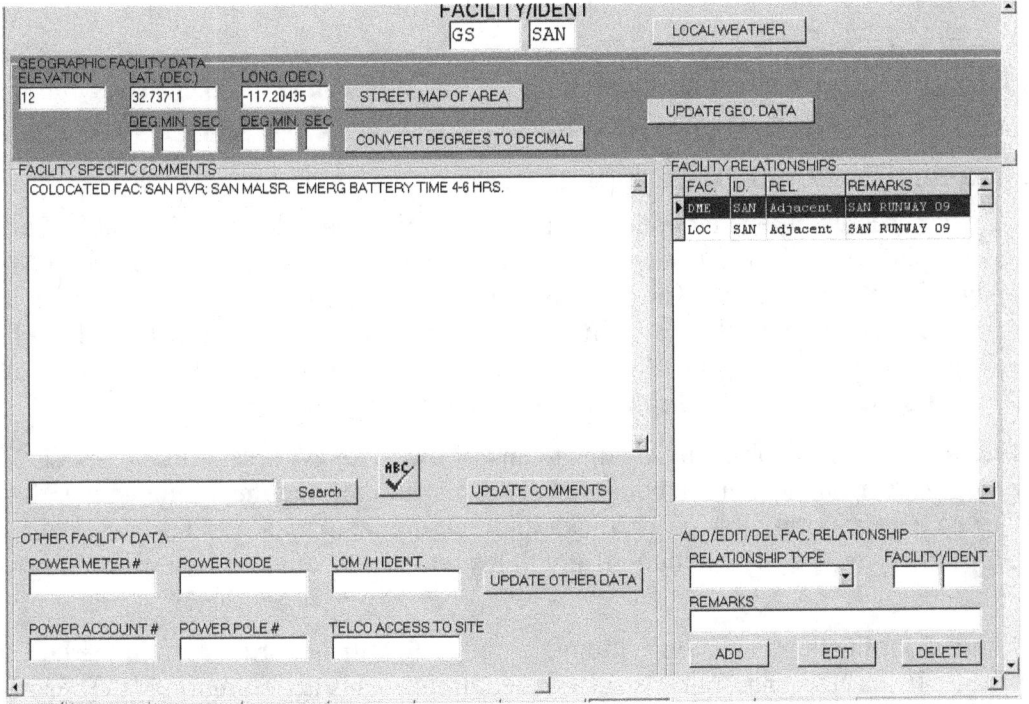

Figure 16e. Event Manager facility information.

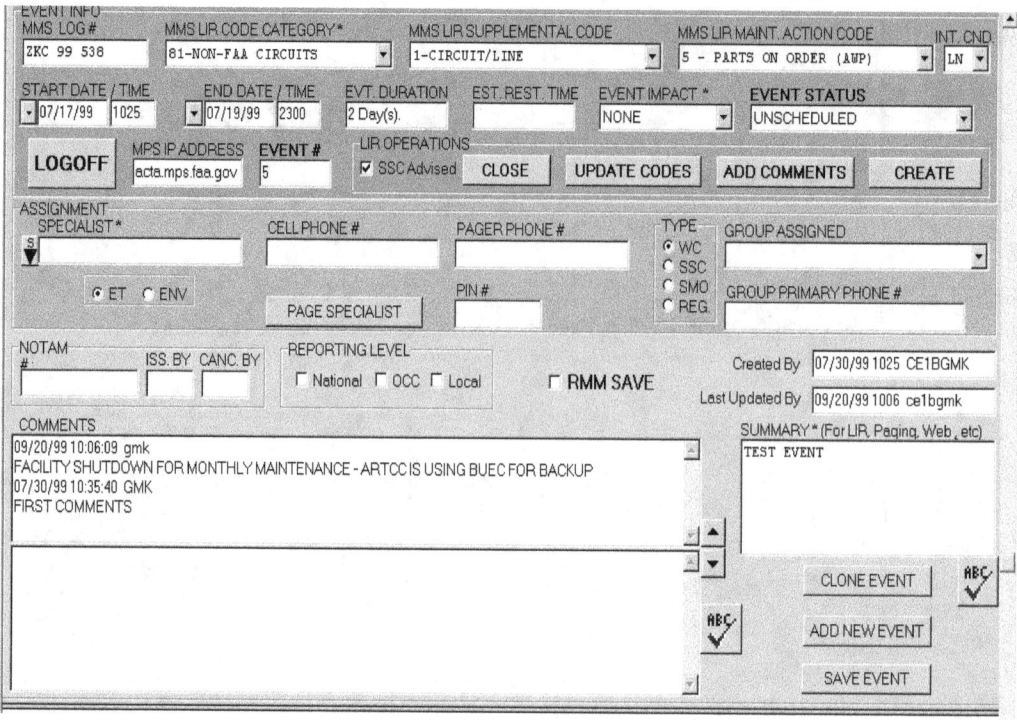

Figure 16f. Event Manager phone book sheet.

2.3.13.1 Event Manager Symbols

Event Manager is a form-and-tables-based program that relies on text rather than symbols. The buttons with which the user interacts are labeled with text rather than graphic images.

2.3.13.2 Event Manager Coding Conventions

Event Manager uses a single letter code together with a color code to indicate status of events in the Events Display view. Table 12 depicts these codes. Besides this convention on the Events Display page, Event Manager provides several other color coding changes. Throughout all the pages, wherever a scrollable list appears in a field, when an item from that list is selected, it becomes highlighted with the same blue as used to highlight an event on the Events Display page. The text in these highlighted rows then switches from black to white.

On the Interruption Entry Form, any change to any of the fields will result in the SAVE EVENT button becoming surrounded with a bold red box. This is to remind the specialist that the event must be saved before exiting this page. In addition, on the Interruption Entry Form page, when the specialist clicks on the SHOW button, any fields that can be queried become highlighted in red.

On the Event Coordination page, when the radio button for final coordination in the Display Options frame is selected, that frame is surrounded in red. This action reminds the specialist that the UPDATE button must be selected for information to be added to the database.

On the Coordinate Information page, the colors red, blue, orange, green, and dark gray are used to define the separate elements of the page itself and have no other purpose. These are the currently defined colors and symbols for the status fields column, labeled Status (ST).

Table 12. Event Manager Event Types and Related Coding Conventions

UNSCHEDULED	Red background with a white letter X	
CLOSED	Blue background with a white letter C	
NOT COORDINATED	Blue background with the white number 1	
PENDING APPROVAL	Blue background with the white number 2	
APPROVED	Blue background with the white number 3	
DISSAPROVED	Dark Gray background with the white letter D	
MCC ONLY	White background with a black letter M	
SPECIAL EVENTS	Orange background with a white letter S	
BATTERY	White background with a black letter B	
ENGINE GENERATOR	Yellow background with the black letter E	
FLIGHT CHECK	Green background with the black letter F	
INFORMATION ITEM	Cyan background with a black letter I	
LINE PROBLEM	Fuchsia background with a black letter L	
RETURNED	Orange background with the black letter R	
VOID	Blue background with the white letter V	
TECHNICAL REQUEST	Red background with a white letter T	

2.3.14 Automated Radar Terminal System

Automated Radar Terminal System (ARTS) is a two-computer-beacon processing system used at terminal control facilities with airport surveillance radar. ARTS II is used primarily at low- to medium-activity airports, and ARTS III is used at high-activity airports. ARTS comes in two forms, E and A. It will remain the primary terminal automation system until it is replaced with Standard Terminal Automation Replacement System (STARS).

ARTS monitoring and control takes place at the TRACON or at the ARTCC. System specialists, technicians, and the NAS/NOM are responsible for monitoring this equipment.

2.3.14.1 ARTS Symbols

Table 13 depicts ARTS symbols. We have separated the table to represent the different applications of ARTS: System Configuration, Software Control, Reports, Maintenance, Function Configuration, Disk Access, ARTS Tools, and Administrative Tools.

Table 13. ARTS Symbols and Meanings

System Config - The System Config group supports the modification of the system configuration parameters and equipment.

	Assume SMS - allows the user to reconfigure the Non-SMS SMC-PC to be the System Monitor Station (SMS)		Site Adaptation - allows the user to enter, modify, verify, and save Site Adaptation parameters and files
	Flight Plan Termination - allows the user to request the termination of specified flight plans		Site Adaptation Data Downloader - provides the user the ability to download Site Adaptation files
	Keyboard & Display Configuration - allows the user to view and/or modify the status of displays and keyboards		Sensor Config - allows a user to view and/or modify the sensor/segment masking settings, automatic switching settings, and radar overload sensing settings
	Processor Config - allows the user to reconfigure and/or reset the SP chassis		Sign On/Sign Off - allows the user to sign on or off one or more keyboard positions and/or request a summary status report
	Resectorization - allows the user to resectorize the fix configuration and/or to request a partial resectorization		System Settings - allows the user to view and/or modify the system Date/Time, Altimeter, and Automated Terminal Information Service/General Service Information (ATIS/GSI) settings
	RSM Config - allows the user to request changes in the status of the Remote System Monitor (RSM) Configuration		

Software Control - The Software Control group contains functions, which support the initialization and software configuration of the ARTS.

	Reinitialize All Displays – allows the user to request the reinitialization of all displays		Software Revision Level – allows the user to view and/or print the Software Version Report for all processors
	Software Downloader – controls the configuration of program and adaptation files for the microprocessor chassis connected to the same network as the SMC-PC host processor		System Reset – allows the user to request a system reset of all SP and DNIP chassis in an ARTS IIE configuration

Table 13. ARTS Symbols and Meanings (Cont.)

Reports - The Reports group contains a collection of ARTS-related reports that can be requested by the user.

	DP Status Report - displays the status of all keyboards and displays in the ARTS system		Recording Status Report - displays recording-related information
	Function Status Report - displays the status and settings of ARTS system functions		RTQC Report - allows the user to request the printing of a Real-Time Quality Control (RTQC) Report
	LAN Status Report - is a report-based application which displays a table containing the status of the LAN (up, down, or not configured) for each network device		Sensor Config Status Report - displays sensor-related information
	MCI Inhibit Region Report - allows the user to request a printout of a list of all keyboards that have an MCI Inhibit Geographical Region(s) enabled, and the MCI Suppressed Region numbers for each keyboard		Subsystem Status Report - allows the user to request the printing of Subsystem Status Reports
	MSAW Inhibit Region Report - allows the user to request a printout of all MSAW General Terrain Monitor (GTM) Regions that are inhibited		System Config Status Report - displays system configuration information (chassis state and peripheral information) for all non-DP chassis
	NID Assignment Report - is a report-based application which displays a table organized by NID of all adapted chassis type assignments		

Maintenance - The Maintenance group contains maintenance applications that provide evaluation, monitoring, testing, and equipment verification for the ARTS hardware.

	Diagnostic Test – initiates resident internal firmware self-tests for user-selected chassis		LAN (Local Area Networks) Test – performs a functional verification of the logic circuitry and data paths associated with the LAN
	DNIP Device Tests – execute in a DNIP that is in the off-line state, and provide the ability to determine the operational capability of the equipment attached to the DNIP		Maintenance Manager – contains maintenance applications which provide evaluation, monitoring, testing, and equipment verification for the ARTS hardware

Table 13. ARTS Symbols and Meanings (Con't.)

Function Config - The Function Config group contains a suite of applications, which controls the status and configuration of ARTS functions.

	Conflict Alert Config – allows a user to modify Conflict Alert related settings		Recording Config – allows the user to specify CDR and PD-PC recording related settings
	CRDA Config – allows a user to view or modify the current Converging Runway Display Aid (CRDA) settings		RTQC Config – allows a user to view and modify the current Real Time Quality Control (RTQC) registration settings
	ILS Monitor Config – allows the user to modify ILS Monitor-related settings		System Function Config – allows the user to enable or inhibit System Functions
	Interfacility Config – allows a user to specify IF related settings		System Monitor Config – allows a user to specify which classes of messages from the System Monitor will be displayed/printed and the printer destination
	MSAW Config – allows a user to modify MSAW related settings. The user can enable or inhibit MSAW, Approach Path Monitor, and one or more MSAW General Terrain Map (GTM) regions		TMS Config – allows a user to modify Traffic Management Information System-related settings
	Performance Monitor Config – allows a user to enable or disable performance monitoring and reporting		

Disk Access

	About Disk Access		FTP		Disk Access Read Me		RPC Information
	Administrator Utility		NTP		DNS Query		Show Mounts
	Disk Access FAQ		Ping		DOS2UNIX		TELNET

	Disk Access Help	
	Remove Disk Access	
	Finger	

46

Table 13. ARTS Symbols and Meanings (Con't.)

ARTS Tools - The ARTS Tools group contains miscellaneous and special-purpose ARTS support functions.

	CDR Editor – provides the user with formatted output of previously recorded CDR data. The user can define or modify input, output, data class, and filter settings		Lat/Long X/Y Calculator – allows the user to convert polar coordinates (latitude and longitude values) to rectangular (X/Y) coordinates, and vice versa
	CDR Time Selected Output – provides the ability to copy CDR data from one CDR file set to a user-specified location, using a user-specified starting and ending date/time		List Directory – displays the contents of a user-specified disk directory in a scrollable text window
	Desktop Toolbar – displays the current system status and allows a user to easily control ARTS applications without having to search for icons or windows by placing selected functional icons in the button bar		Replay – provides the user the ability to replay CDR display data for multiple displays over the network
	Disk Utilities – allows a user to copy, mount, or unmount disks or to build a file system on a disk		Suicide Note Utility – allows the user to view, print, and clear suicide notes
	File Dump – displays the contents of a user-specified file in both hexadecimal and ASCII formats		System Monitor – allows the user to observe a read-only text window that displays system monitor messages as they are received. This dual window also allows the user to enter display keyboard commands
	GNU Plot –supports the plotting of CDR Editor and Site Adaptation generated plot files		

Administrative Tools (Common) - The Administrative Tools group contains system administration and management tools.

	Backup – is a graphical tool for backing up and restoring files, particularly CDR files. This tool may be used to backup or restore any file(s) within the system, including the entire SMC-PC		Remote Access Monitor
	Disk Administrator		User Manager
	Event Viewer		Windows NT Diagnostics
	Performance Monitor		

2.3.15 Standard Terminal Automation Replacement System

Standard Terminal Automation Replacement System (STARS) will replace the existing ARTS. There are two versions of STARS, Early STARS and Full STARS. The Full STARS M&C Workstation displays the status and state of the STARS resources and external interfaces. The initial display includes a Full Service Level (FSL) panel on the upper half of the screen with an Emergency Service Level (ESL) panel on the lower half of the screen. The ESL provides backup if systems in the FSL are offline. Both panels allow for monitoring systems. The title bar for the FSL contains "Full Service Monitoring and Control Position," at the top of the screen. The word Emergency replaces the word for the ESL half of the display. This naming standard (appearing at the top of each window or page) remains constant as operators open additional views in the system to perform monitor and control tasks.

2.3.15.1 STARS Symbols

The STARS M&C interface does not use pictorial, graphical symbols for either Early STARS or Full STARS in ways that have been described for other systems. Instead, it uses a schematic with color-coded text boxes. Users will interact with buttons in the displays that contain text and acronym information, and these buttons will change color to reflect system status. The main page interface of STARS presents a high-level schematic allowing operators to identify and interact with resources as connected in the overall system. Figure 17 displays the Full STARS. Figure 18 displays the Early STARS.

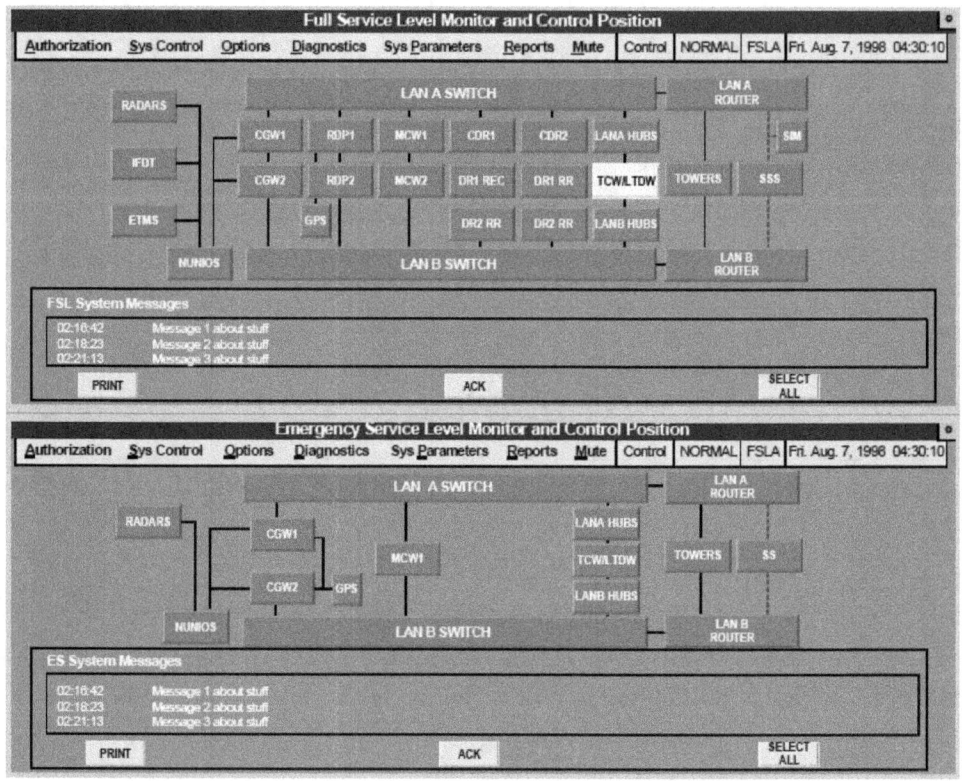

Figure 17. Full STARS.

48

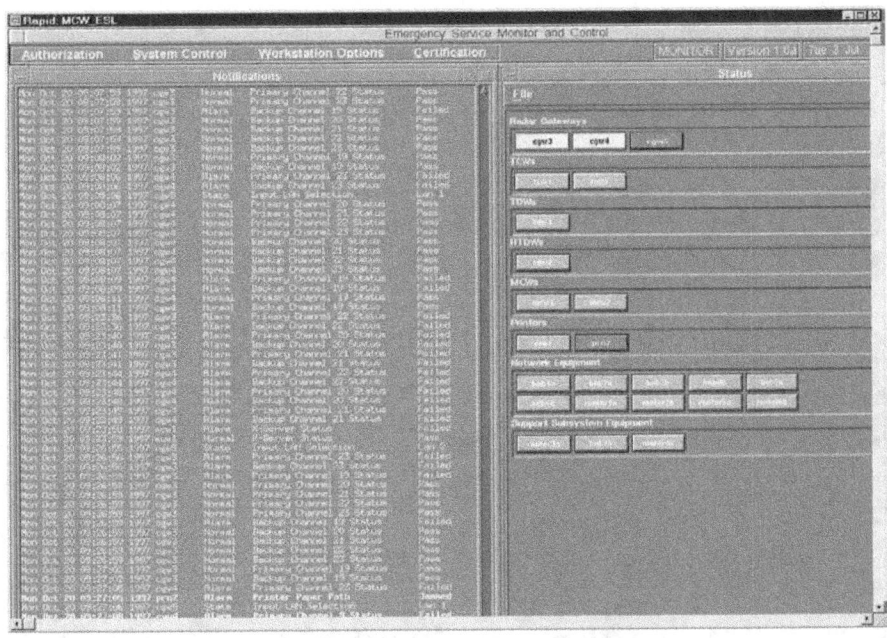

Figure 18. Early STARS - Red flashes until acknowledged means loss of redundancy or critical function.

2.3.15.2 STARS Coding Conventions

Four colors indicate the status of the different systems represented on STARS. Red indicates alarm (a loss of redundancy or critical function); yellow means alert; green means normal; and dark gray means offline. Black text appears on buttons in the alert condition, and white text appears when the normal, alarm, and offline status coding colors are used on buttons. White text also appears in the message window on a gray background. Flashing indicates an unacknowledged alarm/alert.

2.3.16 Random Access Plan Position Indicator

Random Access Plan Position Indicator (RAPPI) is an extension of the Peripheral Adapter Module Replacement Item (PAMRI) system. PAMRI provides the interface between the Host processor and many peripherals including radars and looped system interfaces. Figure 19 shows a view of RAPPI. The RAPPI display provides visual indicators for the radar data currently being received from a radar site. Operators can configure the Main Display RAPPI Menu Item to provide up to 18 radar data sites, if necessary. The main display will present the radar data that are pertinent to an ARTCC. Specialists can click on a particular data display in order to receive detailed information for that radar equipment.

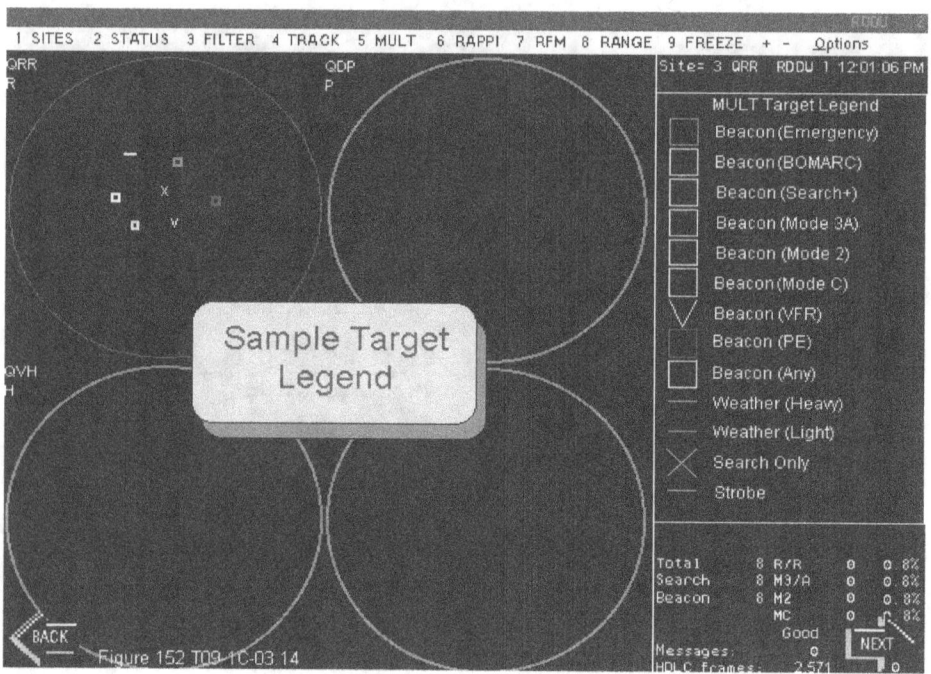

Figure 19. RAPPI with targets.

When the specialist chooses the RAPPI menu item, the specialist interfaces with a display containing a menu bar, the current, maximum-displayed target range, the selected site, the target display circle, selection buttons, search, a text message display area, and channel activity status. Four options appear at the top of the screen: Print, Options, Site/Channel, and Help. The target display circle shows the symbols for any radar targets received from the chosen radar site (see Figure 19). If there are multiple pieces of equipment at a particular location within the range, the equipment symbol with the highest priority appears in yellow. The target legend display area (right side of screen) displays the Target Legend (see Figures 20 a and b) with different RAPPI symbols that can be displayed. To the right of each symbol is the name for that symbol.

2.3.16.1 RAPPI Symbols

The symbols used for RAPPI and their meanings are shown in Figure 20 a and b.

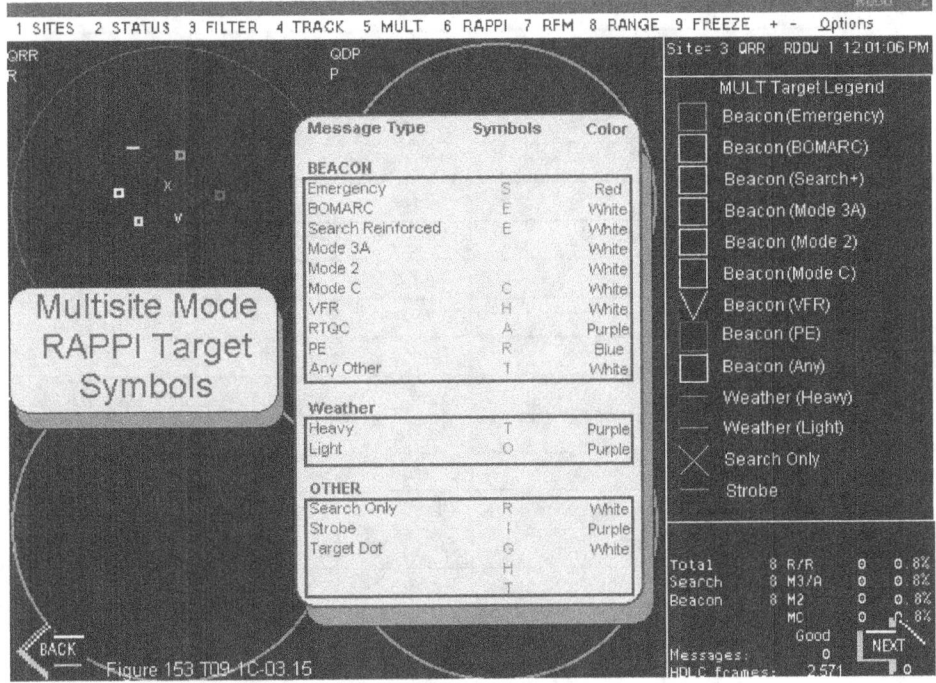

Figure 20a. Multisite mode RAPPI target symbols.

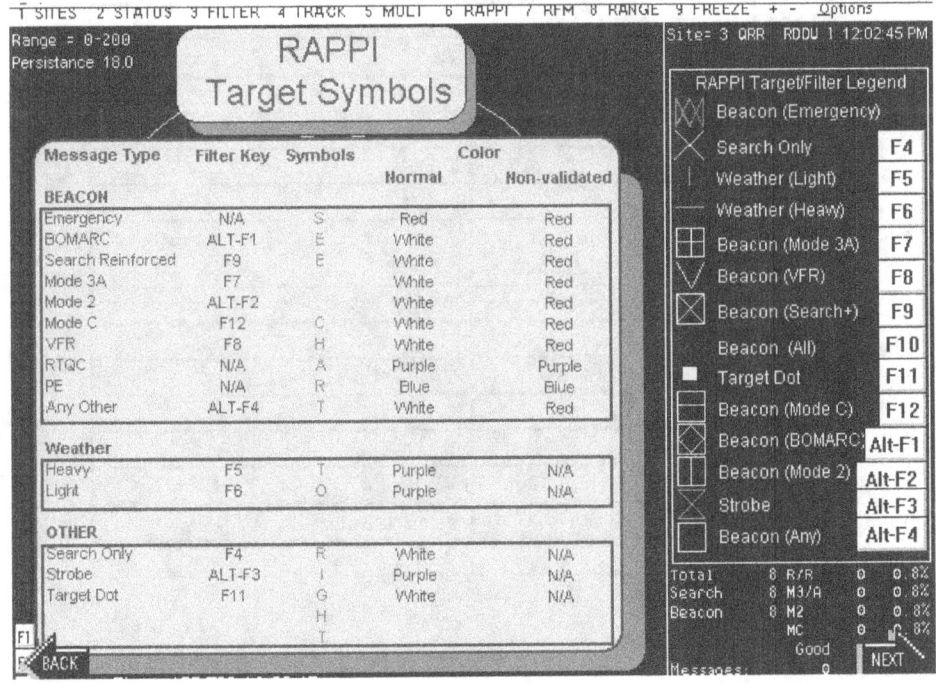

Figure 20b. RAPPI target symbols.

2.3.16.2 RAPPI Coding Conventions

Tables 14 and 15 describe the coding used for RAPPI.

Table 14. Color Conventions Used for Multisite Mode RAPPI Target Symbols

MESSAGE TYPE	COLOR
BEACON Emergency A	Red
BOMARC - A	White
Search Reinforced	White
Mode 3AA	White
Mode 2A	White
Mode CA	White
Visual Flight Rules (VFR)	White
RTQC	Purple
Program element	Blue
Any Other	White
Heavy Dense WEATHER	Purple
Light Scattered WEATHER	Purple
Search Only	Green/White
Strobe	Purple
Target	White (filled)

Table 15. RAPPI Target Legend

MESSAGE TYPE	COLOR
Beacon Emergency	Red
Search Only	White
Weather (light)	Purple
Weather (heavy)	Purple
Beacon Mode 3	Aqua
Beacon Visual Flight Rules (VFR)	Aqua
Beacon Search	White
Beacon All	
Target	White (Filled)
Beacon (Mode C)	White
Beacon (BOMARC)	White
Beacon (Mode 2)	White
Strobe	Purple/Aqua
Beacon Any	White

2.3.17 Enhanced Traffic Management System

Enhanced Traffic Management System (ETMS) provides flight routing information to the controllers. In this system, maps of different regions are displayed with flight traffic overlaid. Various screens pop up to display flight information, weather information, and rerouting information. ETMS also displays distance measurement and runway visual range (RVR) capabilities.

M&C systems for this system are located at AMCCs. From the UNIX-based display screens, specialists can maneuver the directory structure, print files, obtain help, and control display output. The system incorporates symbols with their interfaces, uses pop-up and pull-down menus, and uses frequent command driven interactions in the various pages of these screens.

2.3.17.1 ETMS Symbols

Figure 21 depicts some of the symbols used for ETMS.

2.3.17.2 ETMS Coding Conventions

From the alerts pull-down menu, specialists can set the status of alarms. The system will beep and/or flash for alarms of any alerted element identified with the Alarm Specification dialogue box. Airports, specific 'fixes' (location), and sectors can be specified. An Alarm Parameters box (ReAlerts) specifies alarms for current flights. Alerts can also be chosen for proposed flights. From the Beep Parameter box, the duration and number of beeps/flashes per second can be changed.

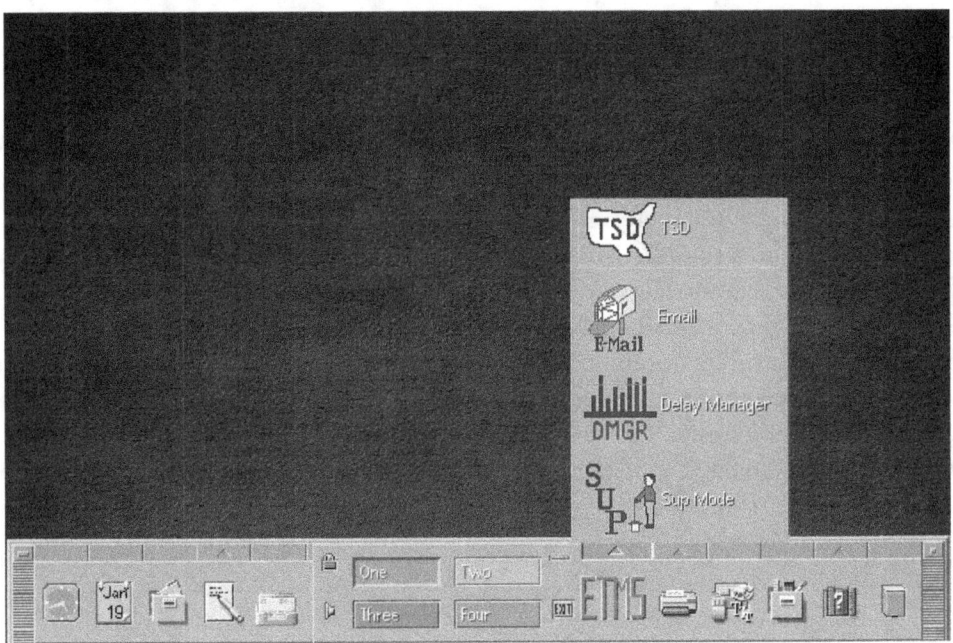

Figure 21. Some of the symbols and a pop-up menu from ETMS.

3. RESULTS

3.1 Symbol Use

Visual symbols served several different functions at the AF sites visited. Most of the visual symbols encountered in normal office work are classified as object icons. These symbols represent objects on a virtual desktop. Like the physical objects they represent metaphorically, these objects can be moved or opened. Only ARTS had symbols that could be considered object icons in that they could be opened or moved. Codex, HOSCR, and HNL had what we classified as atypical object symbols. The symbols in this category are similar to object symbols in that they represent physical objects but may not necessarily be opened or moved. Instead, the user receives additional information about the object (e.g., status of subcomponents of the object) when the user selects these symbols. These symbols are also similar to status symbols in that the background portion of the symbol indicates the status of the object.

DSR and MASS both use symbols to convey status. The use of symbols to convey status is not very common in the office environment. Graphic menus, however, are often encountered in a typical office environment within software programs. The graphic menus sometimes referred to as toolbars or palettes, present small symbols that represent different operations in a menu or toolbar. For example, in a word processing program, a small graphic of a diskette in the toolbar indicates the function "save file." Unlike symbols representing objects on a virtual desktop, items in a graphic menu cannot be directly manipulated by "dragging and dropping" the symbol. Several AF systems used symbols in this way, including some of the symbols in Codex, some of the symbols for MASS, some of the symbols for DVRS, and the symbols for IMCS. One system (RAPPI) used symbols for representation of both object status and location. This use of symbols in this way is similar to the use of graphical symbols on maps or situation displays. RAPPI was the only instance of symbols being used this way observed at the sites visited. Table 16 shows the types of visual symbols used by the various systems.

Several of the systems observed at AF sites do not use conventional graphic images of symbols to represent information on the screen. Instead, these systems use diagrams with color-coded, labeled push buttons, sometimes referred to as 'text boxes.' LDRCL uses the text push buttons to represent commands, whereas DAS/RSD and STARS use the text push buttons to represent objects with color indicating the status of the objects. The text pushbuttons used by STARS and DAS/RSD are atypical of most pushbuttons used in desktop office software in that they represent the status of objects rather than commands (e.g., print or cancel). This affects the applicability of some research and guidelines, which were formulated for symbols used in an office environment. This being said, we will examine the visual symbols collected in this document against applicable human factors design guidance, interpreting the guidelines as necessary to explain how they fit to AF visual symbols.

Table 16. Use of AF Symbols by Different Systems

SYSTEM	SYMBOL USE
ARTS	Object symbols
Codex	Atypical object symbols with some drawing symbols in a graphic toolbar
HOCSR	Atypical object symbols with the background indicating status
HNL	Atypical object symbols with the background indicating status
DSR	Status symbols
MASS	Status symbols and graphic menu
DVRS	Status symbols and graphic menu
IMCS	Graphic menu
VSCS	Text push buttons with some graphic push buttons
LDRCL	Text pushbuttons representing commands
DAS/RSD	Text push buttons representing status of an object
STARS	Text push buttons representing status of an object
RAPPI	Situational display or map-like symbols
Event Mgr	Forms and tables program, has some text pushbuttons, letter and color coding
ODAPS	Single letters indicate status

3.2 Symbol Standardization

The HFDG (DOT, 1996) recommends that human-machine interface designs be standardized to the degree practical and compatible with system functions and purposes. The literature reviewed on symbol design from Lin and Kreifeldt (1992), Lin (1992), Geiselman and Christen (1982), Remington and Williams (1986), and ISO standards documentation (ISO/IEC, 2000a, 2000b) support this statement. Standardization of symbols allows skills, knowledge, and experience from one system to transfer to another system, minimizing the need for additional memorization. Standardization can cut down on learning/training time and, therefore, on cognitive demands. A key tenet of standardization is consistency within and between systems.

Symbols should be consistent within an application and across related applications, including similar graphics and style (Ahlstrom & Longo, 2001). Looking at the variety of different symbols cataloged in this report, it is obvious that there is a great deal of inconsistency in graphics and style between the different systems to which AF specialists are exposed. Systems like STARS and DAS/RSD use text push buttons, ARTS has detailed graphics, MASS has simple graphics, HOSCR has fairly simple graphics but uses thinner lines, and Codex has very simple graphics with thin lines and no opaque fill[1]. The level of detail and degree of realism portrayed by the graphics used varies greatly from system to system, as does the line width used.

Once it has been identified that there are inconsistencies between how systems represent symbols, the next logical question is "Which of these ways is the best way to represent the concepts, objects, or functions?" Unfortunately, there is no easy answer to this question. There are, however, general guidelines that can be applied across the symbol sets. Woodson, Tillman, and Tillman (1992) recommend that symbols provide enough detail to make the symbol recognizable and no more. More complex symbols can take a greater time in order to respond (McDougall et al., 2000). Symbols that are drawn with too much detail or too thin of lines may not be distinguishable when shown at the smaller sizes necessary for graphic menu items. Additionally, some research suggests that simple symbols (discriminable based on only a few features) facilitate visual search much more than complex symbols (Byrne, 1993). Thus, the HFDG recommends keeping the graphics on symbols simple with lines thick enough to ensure that the symbol is distinguishable at all of the resolutions at which it will be viewed (Ahlstrom & Longo, 2001). This would imply that as long as the users can distinguish the symbol, it is preferable to use the simpler representations with a lesser degree of realism. We would recommend verifying the ability of users to distinguish the symbol through testing with representative users.

Symbols should not only be distinguishable but also comprehensible (ISO/IEC, 2000a, 2000b). Comprehensibility of the symbols was not tested in this study. Our observation, however, was that the comprehensibility of many of these symbols is questionable, as the meaning of some of the symbols was not readily apparent. As comprehensibility is critical to the understanding of the symbol meaning, this area warrants additional investigation.

To improve visibility and distinguishability, the areas enclosed within the outline of a graphic icon should be opaque, as filled symbols are more visible than outlined symbols with no fill (Ahlstrom & Longo, 2001). Although most of the systems used symbols with an opaque fill, Codex violates this convention by having transparent internal areas.

3.3 Common Concepts, Functions, and Physical Objects Represented by Symbols

ISO has made an effort to standardize many of the icons used as metaphors for functions or physical objects in an office environment. As part of this effort, they have produced a conceptual framework for developing object icons. This framework involves defining a function, associating it with an object, converting basic units of the object into components of the symbol, and combining the components into a symbol (ISO/IEC, 2000a, 2000b). This model for developing object icons can be useful for the process of AF symbol standardization.

A key concept in developing and standardizing symbols is defining a function. The correlate of defining the function when looking at symbols that are already developed is to specify concepts, functions, or physical objects that are common across systems (Herschler, 1999). We looked at the symbols used in AF and documented in this report to try to identify core concepts, functions, and physical objects that were in common across systems. Some of the commonalities that we

---

1. Note that the appearance of line width depends on the color of the line versus the background that it is seen against. Light lines against a dark background would appear thicker than dark lines against a light background on a computer display screen.

identified were: PRINT or PRINTER, WORKSTATION or CPU, MODEM or PORT, CONNECT, DISCONNECT, SELECT or PICK, REFRESH or RESET, ALARM, ALERT, NORMAL, UNAVAILABLE or UNMONITORED, ACKNOWLEDGE, the concepts of REPORT, CONFIGURE, USERS, and SETTINGS.

As we are not experts in the realm of AF systems, there are probably functions, physical objects, or concepts that we did not identify because of differences in the terminology between systems. Additionally, subtle, yet important differences may exist between items that we considered synonymous (such as Modem and Port) of which we are not aware. We recommend, therefore, that any standardization effort employ representative users to identify similarities and differences between the symbol objects, functions, and concepts.

In some cases, it may be necessary for differences in terminology to exist between systems, primarily because different systems are required to do different things. Subject matter experts can identify these differences. Some examples of items with different terminology for the same thing, but that would have to be verified by users, are the word select (used by STARS) and the graphic "pick" (depicting an ice pick, used by MASS). A second example is the use of the word RESET by DAS/RSD. We believe it has the same function as the "refresh" button depicted by a can of air freshener in MASS.

An important element of consistency among the graphics used for visual symbols is the distinctiveness of the symbols and the components that make up the symbols (Deppa & Martin, 1997). The research team examined how the different systems used by AF specialists represented these concepts and items. Codex, HOCSR, IMCS, MASS, and ETMS each had different representations for the concept Print or Printer. Figure 22 shows the different representations for Print or Printer. This figure also illustrates the differences in level of detail and style described earlier in this report. The commonality between these representations is a rectangular figure representing the printer, and a polygon representing paper or a document coming out of the printer. Any standardization of the printer should exploit these commonalities. Other examples of different symbols being used to encode the same function are illustrated in figures 23, 24, 25.

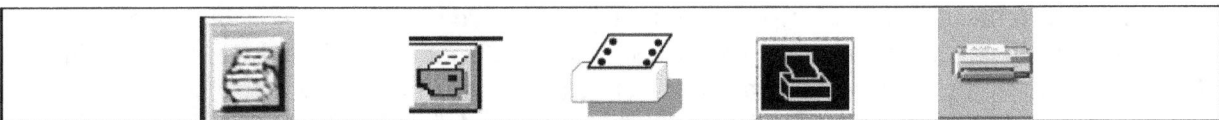

Figure 22. Different examples representing access to the print functions.

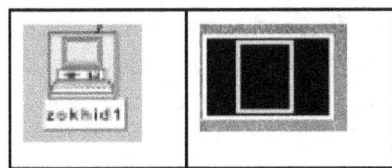

Figure 23. Different representations of CPU/workstation.

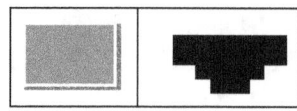

Figure 24. Graphic representation for modem (left) and port (right).

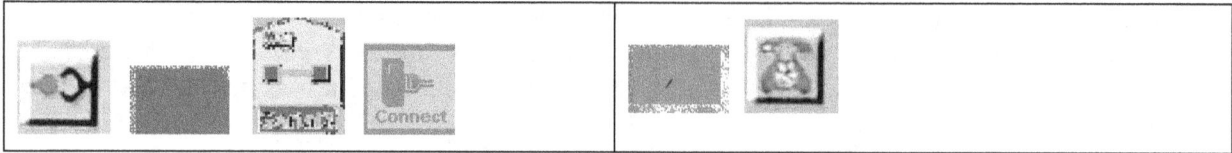

Figure 25. On the left are symbols for connect and on the right are symbols for disconnect (and "hang up" which we believe is analogous).

Appropriate metaphors should be used for the graphic images associated with symbols. The metaphor should make clear the purpose of the symbol. These images may be designed to represent a process or operation literally, functionally, or operationally and should avoid humorous representations (Ahlstrom & Longo, 2001). The metaphor represented by the graphic image in the symbol should be directly related to the functionality it represents (ISO/IEC, 2000a, 2000b). The interpretation of graphic images is influenced by the context in which an image is presented, including the other symbols and images around it (Vukelich & Whitaker, 1993). For this reason, it is preferable to draw from similar metaphors when creating a graphic image for a symbol within a symbol set, and it is important to consider not only the symbol itself, but the symbol within the context of the entire symbol set.

Sometimes the metaphor can cause confusion, especially when the same graphic is used as an analogy for different things. For example, the symbol for a telephone in DVRS is used to indicate a list of telephone recordings. A telephone in Codex indicates dual-dial restoral or single-line restoral. In IMCS, the telephone graphic means hang up a circuit. The HFDG (DOT, 1996), the ISO standards (ISO/IEC, 2000a), McDougall et al. (2000), Ahlstrom et al. (1998), and Blackwell and Cuomo (1991) also recommend that symbols be distinctive. This means a symbol that represents a function, state, or mode should be distinctive in its appearance and be clearly distinguishable from other symbols. Not only should the graphic as a whole be distinctive, but the components of a graphic should have distinctive meanings. In other words, a symbol component should have the same meaning across symbols. A wrench symbol in DVRS indicates setup or the supervisor's options window. In ARTS, the wrench symbol indicates maintenance manager.

By standardizing components of a graphic, the user is able to assign meanings to a class of objects, transferring existing knowledge, reducing training time, and reducing memory load (Herschler, 1999). Simple components can be combined in a symbolic language. Horton (1994) recommends designing a vocabulary of basic symbol components and a grammar of rules for combining these components to make it easier for the user to learn the meaning of the symbols. A simple example of this is the component metaphor for a document. The graphic for a document is a rectangle with greater height than width and a triangle in the top right hand side mimicking a corner folded down. If this graphic is combined with another graphic to indicate the type of document, the user will instantly recognize that the symbol is a type of document. An AF-specific example is the concept of "configure." In ARTS and DVRS, there are nine different instances in which the concept configure is part of what is being represented. Each of these nine instances has a completely different symbol associated with it. If there were a common symbol for the concept "configure," the component for configure could be combined with another component to let the users easily realize that activating this symbol will configure something. This type of component standardization could be greatly beneficial in AF for the concepts of "configure," "report," "settings," and "user." Figure 26 illustrates the idea of "user." These concepts, however, may not be easy to represent graphically. In general, it is easier to represent objects graphically (like report) than actions (like configure). If the action is likely to result in an abstract symbol, consideration should be given to using text instead of a symbol. Abstract icons are likely to be difficult to learn and remember and, thus, should be avoided.

Figure 26. The concept of user is a component of each of these symbols. From left to right, user ID lookup, user history, user manager, view configuration on selected user hard disks.

Some of the concepts that we identified as common across systems are indicated using different symbols and different coding conventions, as illustrated in Table 17. The concept, Alarm, is often represented using color (this is covered more thoroughly in the section on color coding). Sometimes it is represented by a symbol and sometimes by text or a single letter. A red, uppercase 'A' represents an Unacknowledged Alarm condition for MASS; a red, highlighted row or portion of a row represents an Unacknowledged Alarm in IMCS/MMS; and a white 'X' on a red background represents an Unscheduled Event in the Event Manager Status (ST) column. A red triangle represents "down" in DSR. On DAS/RSD, red flashing text represents down, and a bell shape represents down for DVRS. Red color for Codex means "down," "critical status" in HNL, and "failed" for HOCSR. These all appear to be different ways of indicating the alarm status.

Table 17. Representation of Alarm, Alert, Normal, Unavailable, and Acknowledge
by Different Systems

System	Alarm	Alert	Normal	Unavailable /unmonitored	Acknowledge
DSR			Green	Gray	
DAS/RSD	Red/Gray flashing text pushbutton	Yellow text pushbutton	Green text pushbutton	Gray text pushbutton	Text pushbutton "ACK SC" or "ACK ALL"
DVRS	Alarm				
Codex	Red symbol	Yellow symbol	Green symbol		
ODAPS			Letter "O"	Letter "I" - inactive	
HOCSR	Red background shape, Red flashing text in summary list of events	Yellow background shape, yellow flashing text in summary list of events	Green background shape, Green text in summary list of events		Lack of flashing, removal of arrow from left side of summary list of events
HNL	Red background shape	Yellow background shape	Green background shape	Blue background shape	
MASS					
IMCS	Red highlighted text	Yellow highlighted text			
Event Manager					
STARS	Red text push button	Yellow text push button	Green text push button	Gray text push button	

3.4 Text and Labels

Although the use of graphic symbols can save space, speed search, and improve recall and recognition if they are well designed, the use of symbols whose meanings are not clear can make a system more difficult to use (Horton, 1994). Therefore, we recommend that if the function is difficult to represent clearly with a graphic, a text label should be used with the graphic or should replace the graphic. Furthermore, if some ideas can be represented as symbols and others need to be represented as words, the entire array of symbol should use words (Woodson et al., 1992).

If a text label is used with a graphic symbol, label locations and formats should be consistent (Ahlstrom & Longo, 2001). There is a marked lack of consistency in the use of labels on AF system symbols. DVRS labels some, but not all, of the symbols. HOCSR and HNL label all of their symbols. MASS, IMCS, and ARTS have no labels on their symbols. The guidelines specify a symbol should have an identifying label if space permits because, generally, symbols with labels are more meaningful than symbols alone (Guastello, Traut, & Korienek, 1989). If the symbols must be unlabeled, however, users should have a means for displaying identifying information about the symbols.

Critical symbols and symbols within graphic palettes should be labeled unless they are self-explanatory (Ahlstrom & Longo, 2001). Unfortunately, symbols that are used in graphic menus tend to be very small and may not have room for a legible label. The common industry solution for these graphic menu symbols is to use rollovers. A rollover is when a text label appears adjacent to the symbol shortly after the pointer focus is placed on the icon (the pointing device "rolls over" the visual symbol in the graphic menu). We have no information about whether the AF systems use rollovers for their graphic menu items but suggest it as a way to maximize user understanding of the symbol without requiring text to be placed within the small symbol space.

Some numbers and letters used in labels (or text pushbuttons) are easily confusable, such as Z and 2 or O and 0. If both numbers and letters are used in a label or text pushbutton, it is important that the letters and numbers are easily distinguished (Wagner et al., 1997). One example of how to distinguish the numbers and letters is seen in DAS/RSD where the numeral 0 has a line through it, but the letter O doesn't. ODAPS and LDRCL are mainly text-based systems, relying solely on clear alphanumeric characters to convey important information. Both have letters and numbers, yet neither has a clear distinction between confusable characters, specifically O and 0.

In general, when alphanumeric characters are used in labels and text pushbuttons, it is recommended to limit the number of random alphanumeric characters in a string. If the label or pushbutton must use large groups of characters, it is recommended to break down the characters into smaller or more meaningful groups (e.g., creating groups of three to four characters or grouping letters with letters and numbers with numbers) (Wagner et al., 1997). The systems that use push buttons (STARS and DAS/RSD) seem to use groups of three to four characters; however, systems that contain alphanumeric characters in the symbol labels do not consistently comply with this guidance. Codex, for example, can have symbols labeled with a string of more than eight consecutive alphanumeric characters. It would be preferable for these strings of letters to be broken down into groups with three to four letters each. HNL uses a six consecutive character string to identify some items, with a three-letter identifier to indicate the ARTCC followed immediately by three letters indicating system type. Adding a space between the ARTCC identifier and the system indicator would make this six-letter string into two three-letter strings and may facilitate identification.

The HFDG recommends that all push buttons within a window have the same size and shape (DOT, 1996). This is generally the case for STARS and some of the screens of DAS/RSD and was clearly the case for LDRCL. There were some pushbuttons of different sizes, which may possibly be explained as the application of size coding. It appears that there is some use of size coding for these screens, but we did not have information on whether the differences in size were purposeful, with the intent of conveying some meaning, such as indications of importance or frequency of use. Overall, the displays complied with the general principle of simplicity with the screen appearing to be orderly and clutter free and the information presented in consistent, predictable locations. All of the text pushbuttons used a simple, sans serif font, in alignment with the human factors recommendations that typeface should be simple.

There were differences between the systems in the use of capitalization. DAS/RSD, VSCS, and STARS used all capital letters. Early STARS and LDRCL used all lower case letters. Inconsistency in the use of capitalization was also found within systems for HOCSR and HNL. For legibility, labels (and text in pushbuttons) should be displayed consistently in either all capitals or in mixed cases, with the first letter of the word capitalized. For maximum legibility, the character height of the text, depending on viewing distance, should be between 20 and 22 minutes of arc, or, at minimum, 16 minutes of arc (Ahlstrom & Longo, 2001). The justification behind using all capital letters is to maximize the size of the text display to meet legibility height requirements (a capital R is larger than a small r), but there is no clear evidence that favors the use of all capital letters over capitalizing the first letter for speed of recognition (there is also no evidence that this is detrimental). Many of the text boxes contain acronyms for systems being monitored. The letters in these acronyms are all necessarily capitalized. For consistency, it makes sense to use all capital letters in the text boxes if some of the labels will be in all capital letters due to acronym use.

3.5 Coding

3.5.1 Color Coding

Color is one of the most frequently utilized codes for visual symbols. Proper use of color coding can decrease response times and facilitate visual search (Kopala, Refsing, Calhoun, & Herron, 1983).

Many colors have well established meanings, called population stereotypes, such as red for error or failure and yellow for marginal conditions. These meanings should be retained if possible, limiting one meaning per color (Ahlstrom & Longo, 2001). According to conventional associations, red should be used to indicate conditions such as no-go, error, failure, alarm, or malfunction. Flashing red should only be used to indicate emergency requiring immediate action to avert personnel injury or equipment damage. Yellow should be used to indicate marginal conditions, caution, or alert. Green should be used to indicate that it is ok to proceed, normal, satisfactory, or within tolerance status. Blue should be only used for advisory items. If the use of color does not follow well-established meanings or if a color is used for which there is no conventional association, a color key should be readily accessible for the user (Ahlstrom & Longo). Table 18 shows the use of colors with conventional associations in AF systems. Information from AF users should be used to verify that the use of these symbols complies with conventional associations, as terminology differed from system to system.

Table 18. Use of Color Coding by Different Systems

System	Red	Yellow	Green	Blue	Gray
DSR	Warning	Warning	Default color	General Info	Not active
DVRS	N/A	N/A	N/A	Highlighting for selected items	N/A
DAS/RSD	MAINTENANCE and UNAVAILABLE	STANDBY (amber)	ON-LINE		Not monitored
MASS	Alarm	Alert	Return to normal	System state change	
MMS	Macro being enabled	Where information needs to be entered		Informing user of activity taking place or requesting specific action	
Event Mgr	Unscheduled event, technical request	Engine generator	Flight check	Closed, not coordinated, pending approval, approved, void, information item	Disapproved
IMCS	Alarm	Alert	N/A	Background color	
Codex	Down	Degraded	Normal		
VSCS	Emergency	BUEC mode XMTR and RCVR ON (A/G) DA/CA on hold (G/G)	Active function	Function available (turquoise)	Button unassigned or unavailable
ODAPS	N/A	N/A	N/A	N/A	N/A
LDRCL	N/A	N/A	N/A	N/A	N/A
RAPPI	Emergency		Search only	PE	
HOCSR	Failed	Degraded	Normal		Not configured for use
HNL	Critical	Marginal	Normal	Unknown status	
STARS	Alarm	Alert	Normal		Offline

There is no universally agreed upon upper limit for the number of colors to use on a display. However, it is agreed that color should be used conservatively and only if it facilitates user understanding or performance. In general, the total number of colors used should not exceed four for a single alphanumeric screen and seven for a set of related screens (Ahlstrom & Longo, 2001), however, the maximum number recommended tends to be highly task specific. For example, no more than six distinct colors should be used if the user must perform visual search based on color discrimination (Ahlstrom & Longo; Wagner et al., 1997). Most of the AF systems did not use more than six colors, with the exception of Event Manager with 10, and VSCS with 12 different background colors and six different text colors. We did not collect data on the extent to which the colors on these systems can be accurately discriminated. VSCS, for example, has three different shades of gray and has both amber and yellow.

Because not all of the population perceives color the same due to color deficiencies, and ambient lighting and other nearby colors can influence the perception of color, color should be used as a redundant coding technique (DOT, 1996; Wagner et al., 1997). Similarly, users should not have to discriminate small areas based on color (Ahlstrom & Longo, 2001). RAPPI does not seem to follow either of these rules for color coding in that some symbols are distinguishable only by differences in color and the symbols subtend a very small area.

Certain colors should be avoided. Highly saturated colors, particularly from different parts of the spectrum (e.g., saturated red and blue and saturated red and green) can cause unwanted visual effects (Ahlstrom & Longo, 2001). Saturated colors can also be difficult for color deficient people to differentiate, particularly saturated red (ANSI, 1988). Pure blue should also be avoided as can be difficult to read or resolve if it is presented on small objects, text, or thin lines because of a lack of blue sensitive cones necessary for resolving fine details (ANSI). Blue can also be problematic for older adults, especially in combination with shades of yellow (Dyck, Gee, & Smither, 1998). We observed small blue symbols in use for the RAPPI system, which may be difficult for specialists to see.

The contrast between a symbol and background or text and background should be sufficient to enhance color perception, perceived image resolution, and ensure readability of text (Ahlstrom & Longo, 2001). Some of the systems used green text presented on a black or dark background. One study found that correct identification of aircraft call signs at nighttime viewing from ten feet away was only 67% when the text was green compared to over 80% correct for yellow, white and red (Federal Aviation Administration, 2002). However, another study found that color did not matter to readability as long as the text contrast remained the same (Krebs et al., 2002). The readability of the text on these monitors should be verified with representative users at viewing distances consistent with normal operations.

3.5.2 Flash Coding

Flash coding can be used as a means to draw attention to a symbol, effectively reducing the search time (Van Orden, DiVita, & Shim, 1993). Because of its high attention getting abilities, flash coding of visual symbols should only be used to indicate a situation with an urgent need for user attention (Ahlstrom & Longo, 2001). Although individual flash rates carry little absolute meaning, flash rates can carry relative meaning, with a faster flash rate indicating more urgency than a slower flash rate (Wagner et al., 1997). Flashing should avoid rates of between 10 to 25 Hz to minimize the risk of seizures for those with photosensitive epilepsy (DOT, 1996). If text must use flash coding (e.g., the text boxes used for many displays), the flash rate should be 1/3 to 1 Hz with an on/off cycle of 70% (Ahlstrom & Longo). DSR uses flash coding for symbols and for text. These flash rates conform to accepted human factors practice. In fact, the use of bright/dim flashing instead of on/off flashing ensures that the text is always present. We did not have precise flash rates for other systems such as VSCS, STARS, and HOCSR. This information should be collected and used for a future standardization effort. The standard should state when and at what rate an item should flash.

3.5.3 Shape Coding

The use of shape coding facilitates the recognition of warnings and can help support the user's ability to discriminate between categories of icons (Riley, Cochran, & Ballard, 1982). Where geometric shape coding is used and each shape is required to be identified without reference to any other, the number of shapes in the set should ideally be 5 and not normally exceed 15

(Ahlstrom & Longo, 2001). With increasing numbers of shapes, the learning time increases and the ability to recall the meaning decreases (Wagner et al., 1997). Shape coding is a method of coding for the HOSCR, HNL, and DSR systems. DSR uses 5 shapes, whereas HOSCR and HNL use 10 different geometric shapes to enhance the meanings of symbols used on the display. Although HOCSR and HNL are beyond the ideal of 5, they are within the acceptable limit of 15. It should be verified with users that the shape coding used by these systems enhances the information, but it is not critical to the task for users to identify each of these shapes individually.

The shape coding used for alert in DSR is a triangle standing on one point. An equilateral triangle standing on its point has been found to be the preferred shape for warnings signs (Riley et al., 1982), which reinforces the use of this shape for the purpose of an alert. The meaningfulness of the other shapes used by DSR is unclear.

Shapes should be clearly discernable from one another, avoiding similar geometric forms (Wagner et al., 1997). The shapes codes used by HOCSR for network and software are very similar. It seems that it is necessary for users to distinguish between these two items because they were given two different shapes. By looking at these shapes, it appears that these two symbols would be easily confused, but we did not gather empirical data on confusability. The ability of users to distinguish between shapes, the comprehensibility of shapes, and established meanings for the shapes used in AF systems is unknown to us at this time and should be determined as a standardization process progresses.

4. CONCLUSIONS

Currently, AF lacks standardization for symbols across systems. For example, specialists may interact with IMCS/MMS, Event Manager, and MASS in the course of any shift. These systems present similar information and meaning but relay the meaning of information differently, using different symbols and coding conventions. For example, a red, capital 'A' represents an Unacknowledged Alarm condition for MASS, a red, highlighted row or portion of a row represents an Unacknowledged Alarm in IMCS/MMS, and a white 'X' on a red background represents an Unscheduled Event in the Event Manager Status (ST) column. This report documents over 200 unique symbols present in the AF environment. One way to reduce the number of symbols to which AF specialists are exposed is through standardization.

This document represents a first step in a standardization process that takes an integrated look at symbol use in AF systems. We have presented descriptions of the work areas, ambient environments, and systems where human-computer interaction occurs, and we have presented the symbols specialists use during these interactions. We have also presented considerations for the use of visual symbols in the different work operational areas, general guidelines related to visual symbols, and some specific human factors recommendations.

This document contains information on systems found within current MCCs and the symbols and coding conventions used by these systems. It follows up by providing a comparison of the current symbol use against human factors best practices as established in research literature, standards, and guidelines. It gives examples of inconsistent symbol use along with explanations.

The next step in a standardization process should be to gather data from users. Users can provide valuable information on the functional definitions of the meanings for the symbols presented in this document. For example, users can clarify if the difference between Port and Modem are significant or whether they are simply two different ways of saying the same thing.

The pre-existing knowledge of the end user group should also be considered when standardizing symbols or developing new symbols. This is another area where users can provide valuable information. There may be some symbols that have become so well known to the users that it would be difficult for users to attribute a different meaning to the symbol. Special care should be taken when dealing with these historical effects. The tradeoffs of teaching new (possibly better designed) symbols or meanings to existing specialists against benefit of new symbols on new and future users should be weighed. In any effort toward interface standardization, symbols with established meanings should be identified, and, where possible, these meanings should be retained. Determining how strong the history effect is for current symbols is beyond the scope of this paper but should be looked at in any standardization effort.

In this study, we have found that there is a great deal of inconsistency in symbol use and in the degree of symbol fidelity. Users, along with human factors experts and experts from other relevant technical areas, can work together to determine general parameters for future symbols such as what fidelity should be used in the representation of symbols in the AF environment. Using this document as a starting point, users and human factors specialists can determine whether the use of a visual symbol is preferable to text for the different circumstances.

Further investigation is needed on the use of coding, including flash coding. A standard on symbol use will need to specify under what circumstances different types of coding should be used on AF systems.

Further investigation is also needed in the area of comprehensibility or learnability of the symbols. We did not collect any data on this aspect of the symbols, but data of this sort are necessary to determine symbol effectiveness.

As a result of this study, we present several recommendations. We recommend that the overall number of symbols be decreased, where possible, through standardization of symbols across systems and possibly by adding labels to some of the symbols. To accomplish standardization, we recommend that human factors experts together with AF users and other technical experts work together to further identify commonalities in function, objects, and concepts that are represented by the symbols and coding conventions contained in this document. We recommend that these parties come to an agreement on the level of realism and style that will be used for graphic symbols used on AF systems. We recommend that any proposed standard symbols be tested against existing symbols for comprehensibility.

Relevant human factors guidelines are contained within this document, along with an initial set of common functions, objects, and concepts. We recommend using the information provided on commonalities in this report as a starting point for a standardization effort. Furthermore, we recommend that the guidelines presented in this document be used to set a framework for the solutions proposed in a standardization effort.

References

Ahlstrom, V., Cranston, R. L., Mogford, R., Ramakrishnan, A., & Birt, J. (1998). *Symbol standardization in Airway Facilities* (DOT/FAA/CT-TN98/20). Atlantic City International Airport, NJ: DOT/FAA William J. Hughes Technical Center.

Ahlstrom, V., & Longo, K. (2001). *Human factors design guide update (Report Number DOT/FAA/CT-96/01): A revision to chapter 8-computer human interface guidelines* (DOT/FAA/CT-01/08). Atlantic City International Airport, NJ: DOT/FAA William J. Hughes Technical Center.

ANSI. (1988). *American national standard for human factors engineering of visual display workstations.* Santa Monica, CA: The Human Factors Society.

Blackwell, J. S., & Cuomo, D. L. (1991). Evaluation of a proposed space and missile warning symbology standard for graphical displays. *Proceedings of the Human Factors Society 35th Annual Meeting* (pp. 102-106).

Byrne, M. D. (1993). Using icons to find documents: Simplicity is critical. *INTERCHI 1993 Conference Proceedings* (pp. 446-453).

Department of Transportation. (1996). *Human factors design guide: For acquisition of commercial-off-the-shelf subsystems, non-developmental items and developmental systems* (DOT/FAA/CT96-01). Atlantic City International Airport, NJ: FAA Technical Center.

Deppa, S., W., & Martin, B. J. (1997). Human factors behind the improved ANSI Z535.3 label standard for safety symbols. *Proceedings of the HFES 41st Annual Meeting* (pp. 816-820). Santa Monica, CA: Human Factors and Ergonomics Society.

Duncanson, J. P. (1994). *Visual and auditory symbols: A literature review* (DOT/FAA/CT-TN94/37). Atlantic City International Airport, NJ: FAA Technical Center.

Dyck, J. L., Gee, N. R., & Smither, J. A. (1998). The changing construct of computer anxiety for younger and older adults. *Computers in human behavior, 14*(1), 61-77. UK: Elsevier Science, Ltd.

Federal Aviation Administration. (2002). *Remote ARTS color display human factors assessment.* Unpublished manuscript, available from the National Airspace System Human Factors Group (ACB-220). Atlantic City International Airport, NJ: DOT/FAA William J. Hughes Technical Center.

Geiselman, R. E., & Christen, F. G. (1982). Perceptual discriminability as a basis for selecting graphic symbols. *Human Factors, 24*(3), 329-337.

Green, P., & Pew, R. W. (1978). Evaluating pictographic symbols: An automotive application. *Human Factors, 20*(1), 103-114.

Guastello, S. J., Traut, M., & Korienek, G. (1989). Verbal versus pictorial representations of objects in a human-computer interface. *International Journal of Man-Machine Studies, 31,* 99-120.

Herschler, D. A. (1999). Tactical display symbology for surveillance operators. In *Proceedings of the 4th Annual Symposium and Exhibition on Situational Awareness in the Tactical Air Environment* (pp. 7-12).

Horton, William (1994). *The icon book.* New York: John Wiley & Sons, Inc.

Hovey, C. K., & Berson, B. L. (1987). Evaluation of ASW tactical symbology. *Proceedings of the Human Factors Society 31st Annual Meeting* (pp. 1403-1407).

International Organization for Standards/International Electrotechnical Commission. (2000a). *Information technology - user system interfaces and symbols - icon symbols Part 1: Icons - general* (ISO/IEC 11581-1). Switzerland: ISO Copyright Office.

International Organization for Standards/International Electrotechnical Commission. (2000b). *Information technology - user system interfaces and symbols - icon symbols Part 2: Object icons* (ISO/IEC 11581-2). Switzerland: ISO Copyright Office.

Kirkpatrick, M., Dutra, L. A., Lyons, R. A., Osga, G. A., & Pucci, J. J. (1992). Tactical symbology standards. *Proceedings from HFES 36th Annual Meeting* (pp. 1087-1091).

Kline, T. J., Ghali, L. M., & Kline, D. W. (1990). Visibility distance of highway signs among, young, middle-aged, and older observers: Icons are better than text. *Human Factors, 32*(5), 609-619.

Kopala, C. J., Refsing, J. M., Calhoun, G. L., & Herron, E. L. (1983). *Symbology verification study.* Wright-Patterson AFB, OH: Flight Dynamics Laboratory, Air Force Systems Command.

Krebs, W. K., Xing, J., & Ahumada, A. J. (2002, September). A simple tool for predicting readability on a monitor. *Proceedings from HFES 46th Annual Meeting.*

Leonard, S. D. (2000). To do or not to do: Both are the questions. *Proceedings of the IEA 2000/ HFES 2000 Congress* (pp. 786-789).

Lin, R. (1992). An application of the semantic differential to icon design. *Proceedings of the Human Factors Society 36th Annual Meeting* (pp. 336-340).

Lin, R., & Kreifeldt, J. G. (1992). Understanding the image functions for icon design. *Proceedings of the Human Factors Society 36th Annual Meeting* (pp. 341-345).

McDougall, S. J. P., deBruijn, O., & Curry, M. B. (2000). Exploring the effects of icon characteristics on user performance: The role of icon concreteness, complexity, and distinctiveness. *Journal of Experimental Psychology: Applied, 64,* 291-306.

Remington, R., & Williams, D. (1986). On the selection and evaluation of visual display symbology: Factors influencing search and identification times. *Human Factors, 28*(4), 407-420.

Riley, M. W., Cochran, D. J., & Ballard, J. L. (1982). An investigation of preferred shapes for warning labels. *Human Factors, 24*(6), 737-742.

Van Orden, K. F., DiVita, J., & Shim, M. J. (1993). Redundant use of luminance and flashing with shape and color as highlighting codes in symbolic displays. *Human Factors, 35*(2), 195-204.

Vukelich, M., & Whitaker, L. A. (1993). The effects of context on the comprehension of graphic symbols. *Proceedings of the Human Factors and Ergonomics Society 37th Annual Meeting* (pp. 511-515).

Wagner, D., Snyder, M., Dutra, L., & Dolan, N. (1997). *Symbol development guidelines for Airway Facilities* (DOT/FAA/CT-TN96/03). Atlantic City International Airport, NJ: DOT/FAA William J. Hughes Technical Center.

Wolff, J. S., & Wogalter, M. S. (1998). Comprehension of pictorial symbols: Effects of context and testing methods. *Human Factors, 40*(2).

Woodson, W. E., Tilman, B., & Tilman, P. (1992). *Human factors design handbook* (2nd ed.). New York: McGraw-Hill.

Young, S. L., & Wogalter, M. S. (2000). Predictors of pictorial symbol comprehension. *Proceedings IEA 2000/HFES 2000 Congress* (pp. 294-297).

Acronyms

A/G	Air/Ground
AF	Airway Facilities
AFSS	Automated Flight Service Stations
AMCC	Air Route Traffic Control Center Maintenance Control Center
ARTCC	Air Route Traffic Control Center
ARTS	Automated Radar Terminal System
AT	Air Traffic
ATC	Air Traffic Control
COTS	Commercial-Off-The-Shelf
CRDA	Converging Runway Display Aid
CTS	Coded Time Source
DARC	Direct Access Radar Channel
DAS	Data Acquisition Subsystem
DAT	Dynamic Address Translation
DCC	Display Channel Complex
DP	Display Processor
DSR	Display System Replacement
DVRS	Digital Voice Recording System
EDARC	Enhanced Direct Access Radar Channel
ERMS	Environmental Remote Monitoring Subsystem
ESL	Emergency Service Level
ETMS	Enhanced Traffic Management System
FAA	Federal Aviation Administration
FDDI	Fiber Distributed Data Interface
FSL	Full Service Level
G/G	Ground/Ground
GMCC	General Maintenance Control Center
GTM	General Terrain Monitor
HID	Host Interface Device
HNL	HID/NAS/LAN
HOCSR	Host and Oceanic Computer System Replacement
HSP	High Speed Printer
ICDA	Integrated Cache Disk Array
ILS	Instrument Landing System
IMCS	Interim Monitor and Control Software
I/OT (or IOT)	Input/Output Terminal
LAN	Local Area Network
LDRCL	Low Density Radio Communications Link
LINCS	Leased Interfacility NAS Communication System
M&C	Maintenance and Control
MASS	Maintenance Automation Software System
MCF	Monitoring and Control Function
MCI	Mode C Intruder
MMS	Maintenance Monitoring System
MPES	Maintenance Position Equipment Subsystem

MSAW	Minimum Safe Altitude Warning
NAS	NAS Area Specialist
NAS	National Airspace System
NOM	NAS Operations Manager
ODAPS	Oceanic Display and Planning System
PCS	Power Conditioning System
PTT	Push To Talk
PVD	Plan View Display
RAPPI	Random Access Plan Position Indicator
RCE	Radio Control Equipment
RCL	Radio Communications Link
RCVR	Receiver
REM	Ring Error Monitor
RES	Ring Error Status
RMM	Remote Maintenance Monitoring
RMMS	Remote Maintenance Monitoring System
RSD	Real-time Status Display
RSM	Remote System Monitor
RTQC	Real-Time Quality Control
SE log	Support Equipment Log
SMC	System Monitoring Console
SMS	System Monitor Station
SP	System Processor
STARS	Standard Terminal Automation Replacement System
TIMS	Telecommunications Information Management System
TMS	Traffic Management System
TRACON	Terminal Radar Approach Control Facility
UNMON	Unmonitored
UTIL	Unselected Frequency (A/G), Idle DA call (G/G), Idle test
VOR	Very High Frequency Omni- Directional Range Radar
VFR	Visual Flight Rules
VSCS	Voice Switching and Control System
VTABS	VSCS Training and Backup System
WARP	Weather and Radar Processor
WSI	Weather Services International
XMTR	Transmitter

Appendix A - Sites Visited

Sites Visited

Leesburg AMCC

The Leesburg AMCC is located adjacent to the eight radar bays on the work area floor. Six to nine thousand aircraft can pass through this region on any given day, making it the fifth busiest region in the NAS. Figure 1 depicts the Leesburg AMCC floor layout.

The array of monitors and lamps near several of the workstations provide illumination. Although we didn't measure the exact lighting level, the AMCC operators' area is very dark as it is located in close proximity to the Air Traffic Control (ATC) work area.

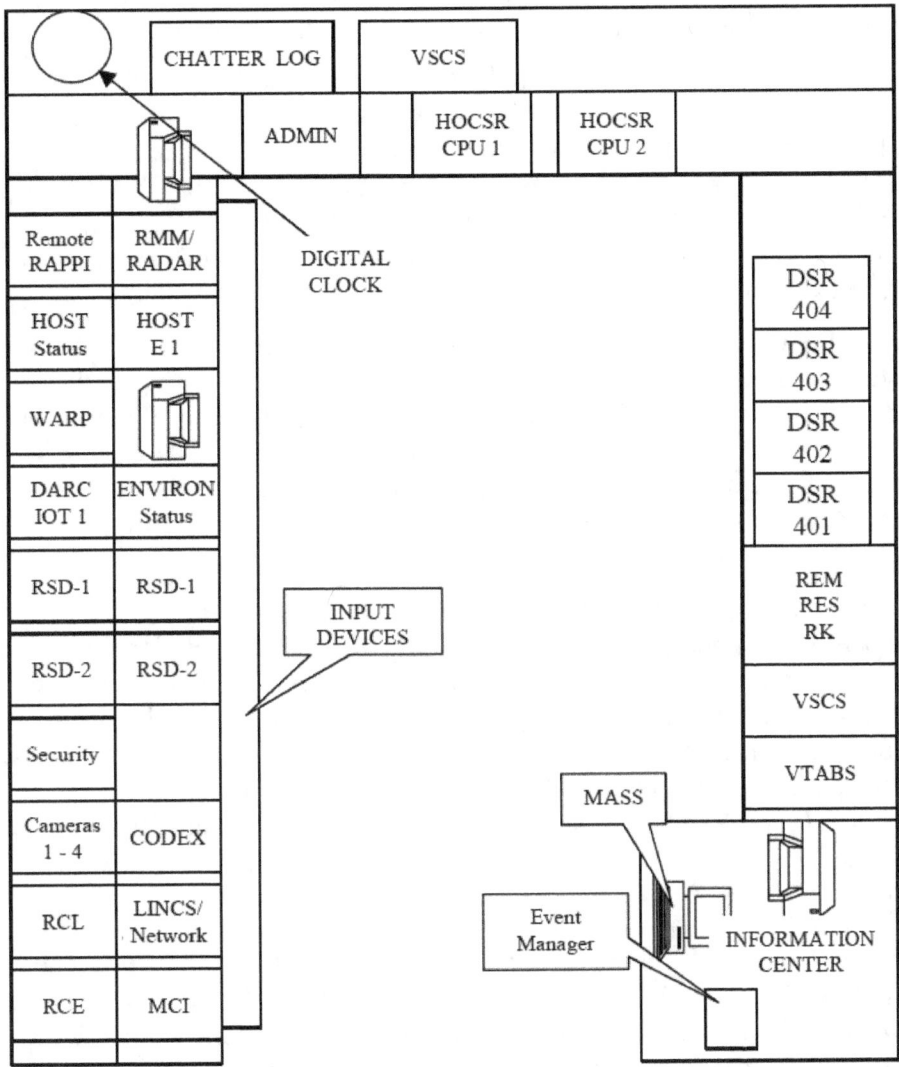

Washington Center – Leesburg, Va. AMCC

Figure 1. Layout: Leesburg AMCC (approximately 18 ft x 25 ft).

AF specialists have chairs strategically located near several of the system monitors. However, the specialists do not remain in one place for any length of time. In order to address a status change from a system, they must move to a particular display. The only exception to this is the real-time status displays (RSD) used with Data Acquisition Subsystem (DAS). When an alarm occurs within one of the systems monitored with DAS/RSD, it is visible from across the work area.

Many systems in the AMCC/GMCC present alarms both aurally and visually. Audible alarm information is beyond the scope of this document. However, where possible, we have provided information necessary for the reader to know which systems provide both types of information.

No fewer than 30 screens display information on the status of the Leesburg facility. Upon entering the AMCC work area, the Information Center workstation is to the immediate right. Event Manager software is running here along with a display for Maintenance Automation Software System (MASS), a monitor with the Weather and Radar Processor (WARP) displayed, the equipment to interact with the Voice Switching and Control System (VSCS), and the VSCS Training and Backup System (VTABS). There is also a hard copy index of acronyms used in the FAA systems with an explanation of their meanings.

To the left and above the workstation are a Ring Error Monitor (REM), the power grid, and the power switching station for the modems. To the left of this workstation and along the right wall of the overall area are the four 28-inch diagonal monitors and input devices for the Display System Replacements (DSR). The back wall of the work area contains two Host and Oceanic Computer System Replacement (HOCSR) workstations, an Administration workstation, a VSCS monitor, and a chatter log monitor. These are placed on two shelves with the workstations below.

The left wall of the work area contains monitors for the Random Access Plan Position Indicator (RAPPI), the Host computer system, an additional WARP, Direct Access Radar Channel (DARC), four RSD monitors, two building security video monitors, the Radio Communications Link (RCL), and the Radio Control Equipment (RCE). On a separate shelf below these monitors are workstations for Remote Maintenance Monitoring (RMM), Host, environmental status, RSD 2, Codex - an event management system from Motorola, Leased Interfacility NAS Communication System (LINCS), and Mode C Intruder (MCI). Additionally, this work area contains three printers.

New York ARTCC

Three specialists were on duty at the New York AMCC, with a fourth as a backup. Their ages were between 40 and late 50. Overall the work area is dimly lighted. Several fluorescent bulbs over the printers in the back of the area provided most of the illumination. Similar to the Leesburg facility, specialists had to move around the workspace to monitor the various systems. Figure 2 shows the floor plan for the New York AMCC.

The main wall of displays contains 27 monitors in nine columns, with a table for input devices below. The monitors are placed in a custom-made unit. The lower row of monitors is perpendicular to the ground, with the mid and upper rows facing downward at slightly increasing angles for easier viewing. Although the angle of the monitors facilitated viewing to some extent, when operators interacted with these displays, they still had to stand and move to them. They then look up and stand away from the 'wall' to view the information on the top monitors.

MASS/Monitoring and Control Function (MCF) is available at the main information desk. However, the RMM located in the bottom row of the fifth column of displays is the system used most often for message traffic by this facility.

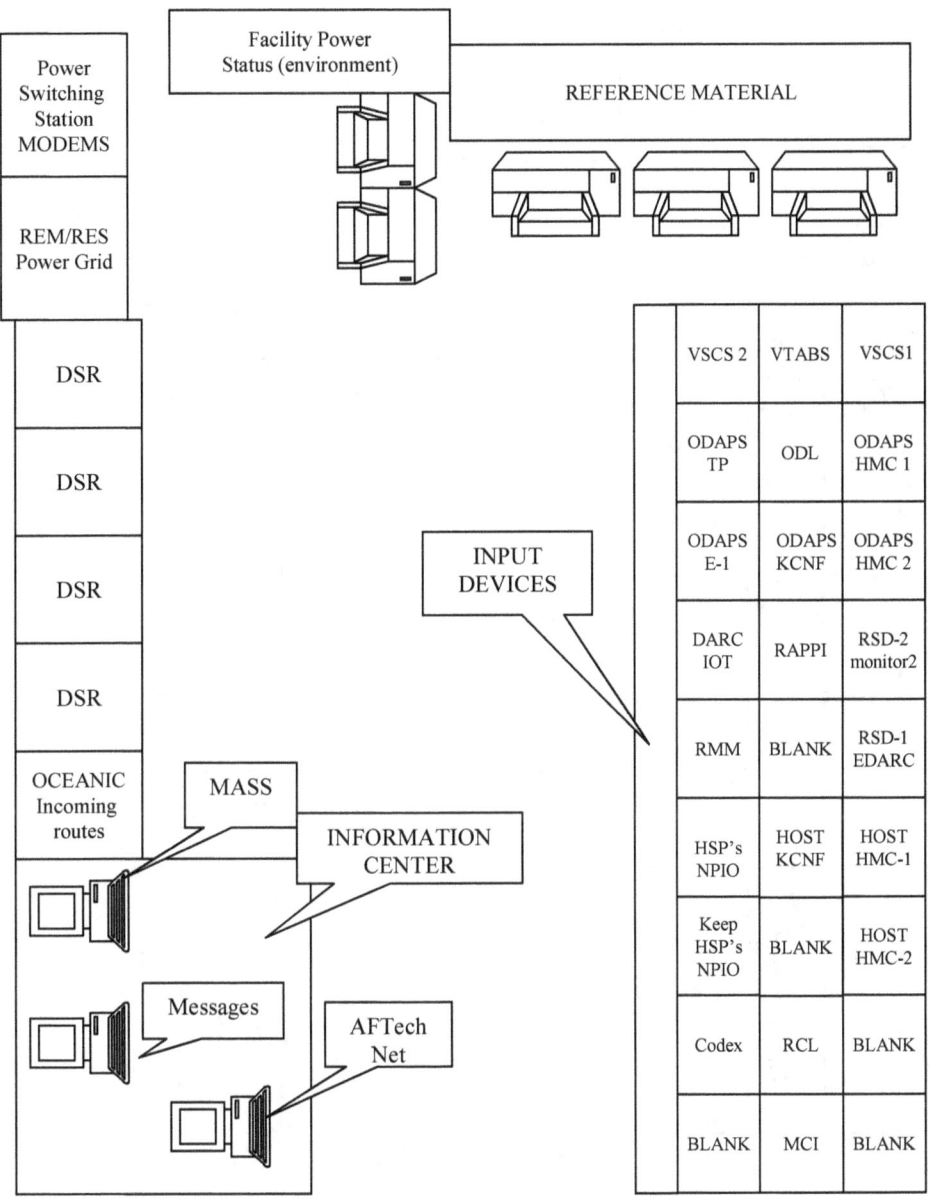

New York Center – Ronkonkoma, NY AMCC

Figure 2. Layout: New York AMCC (approximately 22 ft x 35 ft).

Cleveland AMCC

There were four specialists on duty at the Cleveland AMCC. Their ages range from 35 to 62. As with other AMCC visits, these personnel had prior field experience in various FAA-related systems. Figure 3 depicts the layout of Cleveland AMCC.

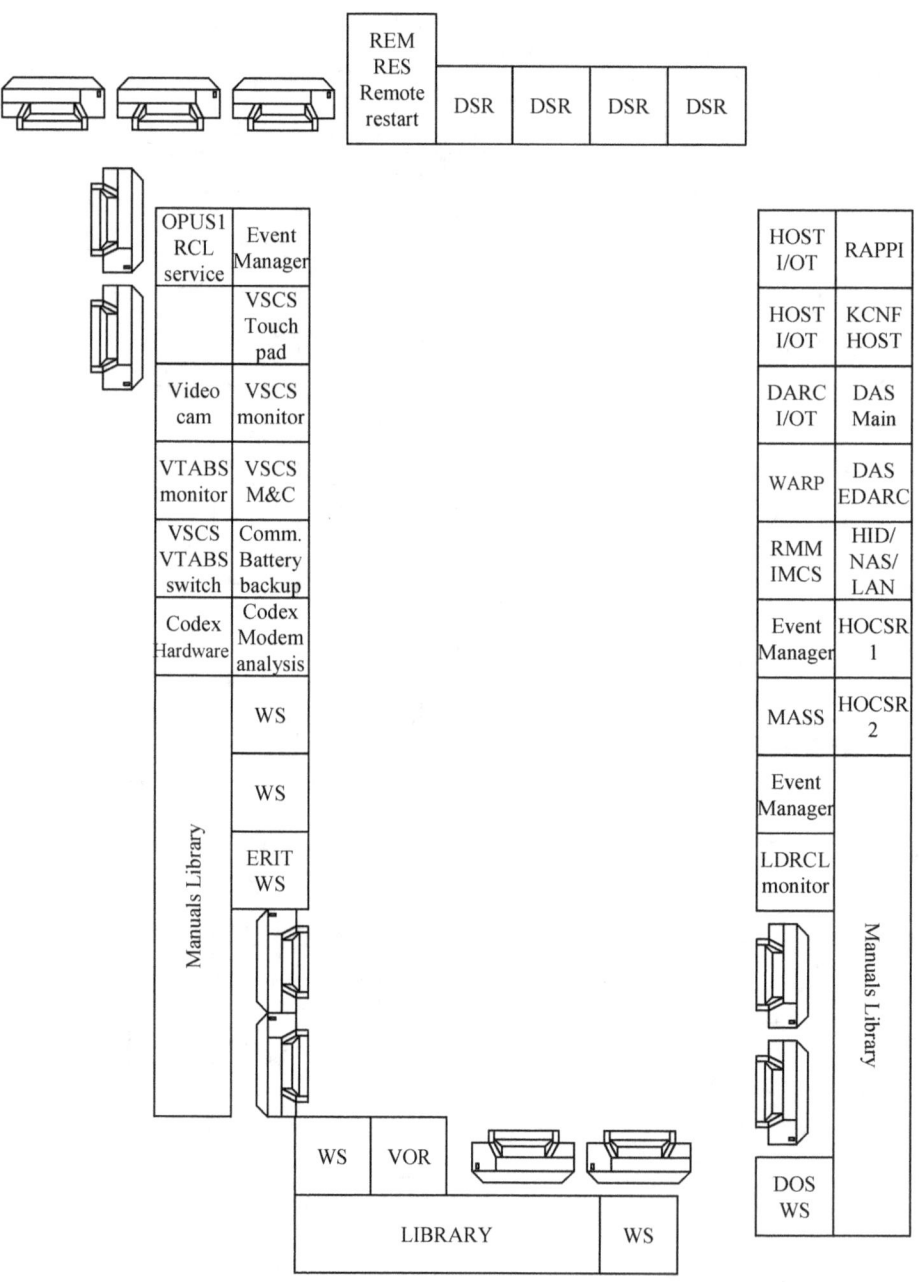

Cleveland Center – Oberlin, Oh.

Figure 3. Layout: Cleveland AMCC (approximately 22 ft x 42 ft).

There are approximately 17 different systems for M&C at this AMCC, which is very well lighted. The DSR consoles are set up at the front of the area, blocking enough of the overhead fluorescents to make those displays very visible for the full length of the work area. Event Manager and a program named Opus 1 are continuously on view and frequently in use. Event Manager is the message relay in this lab, available at four different workstations. One station, where a chair was always in position, had Event Manager centered between MASS on the right and RMM. The systems and equipment monitored at this facility are similar to other AMCCs. VSCS and VTABS take up five positions (including the touch pad interface) to the left of the main work area.

Cleveland AMCC uses Opus, which appears to be unique to this facility. Opus is capable of displaying information from several systems. The researcher observed that it was in constant use at several different locations. The personnel reported that they really like this piece of software.

The equipment room communications area monitors VSCS and maintenance and control for that system mostly takes place there unless the position is unmanned. System testing uses VTABS. Tests are run via VTABS to ensure that the switching equipment is running properly. This area also has an Opus software system.

The AMCC in Cleveland has yet to receive Digital Voice Recording System (DVRS) equipment. Their system provides hard alarms at the equipment itself or personnel make phone calls to describe problems. The M&C personnel have to move to the equipment to interface with it. The equipment has separate touch-pad displays that are beyond the scope of this paper; however, this equipment requires more human interaction than DVRS. For example, DVRS will store communications for up to 15 days and then erase the information. Whereas, the Cleveland system tapes must currently be manually switched and stored each evening.

Boston AMCC

The Boston AMCC is laid out in a square, somewhat separated from the radar floor, approximately 22 ft x 22 ft. For this particular shift, two specialists were on duty. This area was better lighted than the facilities in Leesburg and New York but not as well lighted as Cleveland.

This facility has the same systems as the other AMCCs with the exception of Automated Radar Terminal System (ARTS). HOCSR, Host Interface Device/NAS/Local Area Network (HNL), and MASS are new and only used sparingly at this time. At this facility, Host occupies four monitors with two providing redundancy.

As at the Cleveland AMCC, VSCS is monitored in the equipment room and maintenance and control for that system mostly takes place there unless the position is unmanned.

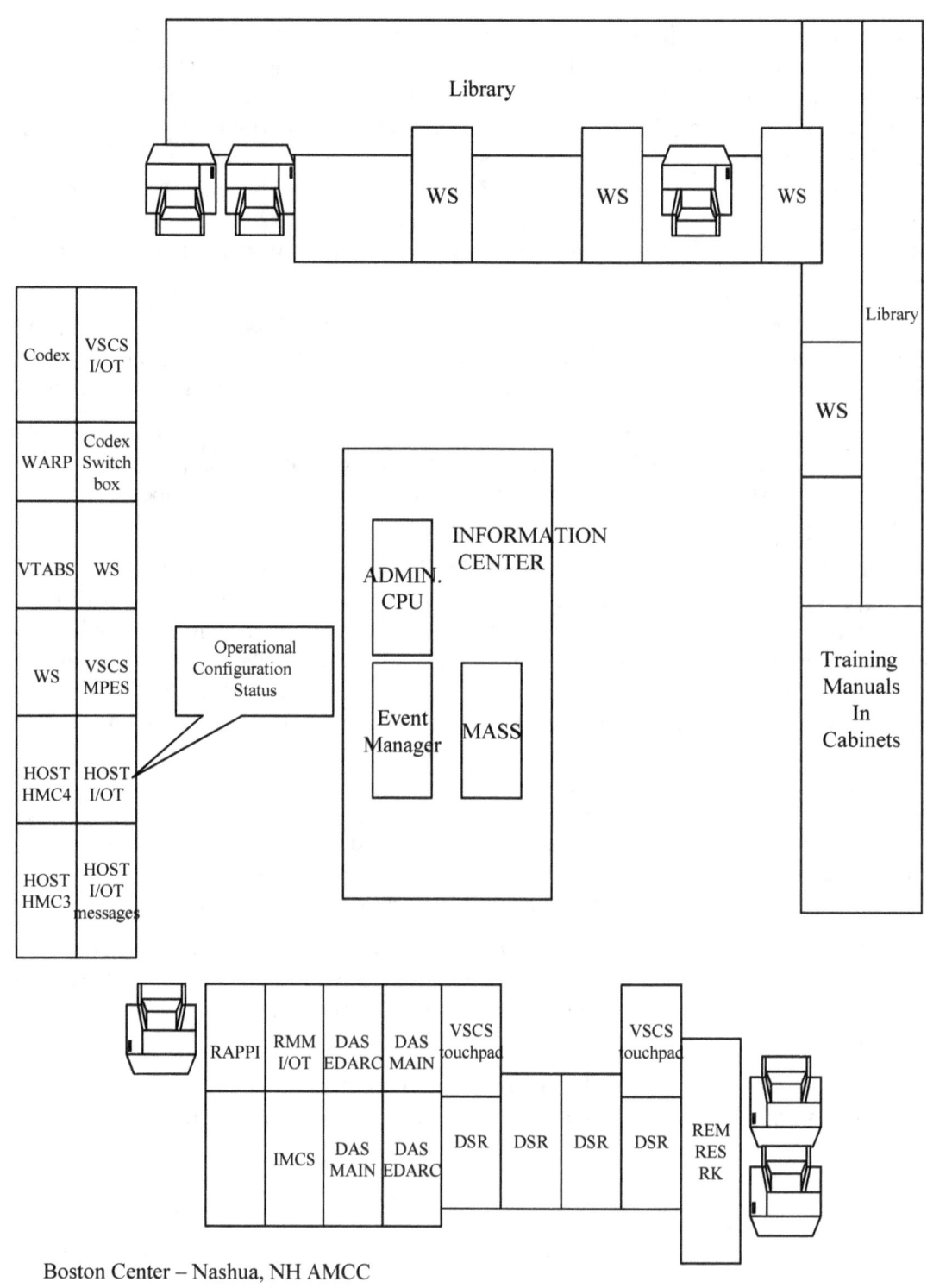

Figure 4. Layout: Boston AMCC (approximately 22 ft x 22 ft).

Leesburg GMCC

The Leesburg GMCC is located in its own room. It is very well lighted with fluorescent ceiling lights and additional task lighting available at each workstation. The walls and dividers are light in color, and this added an additional sense of brightness but not glare. The specialists at this facility remain at their respective workstation and are each involved with three or four information displays. Additionally, two large monitors are suspended from the ceiling (one dedicated to MASS, the other dedicated to WARP), visually accessible from each station with a quick, slight, upward glance. Specialists can address status change from a system from their chairs. See Figure 5 for a layout of the Leesburg GMCC.

A four-person team staffs the Leesburg GMCC. These four positions include the scheduling station, the coordinator station, the supervisor, and the monitor position for the shift. The scheduling station maintains information on arranged outages and flight checks. When necessary, this position responds to trouble calls from the field. This position performs administrative duties on a computer and uses the AF website AFTechNet to help clarify information due to different terminology used at different facilities. A WARP monitor and computers with MASS and Event Manager are also used at this station.

The coordinator station has a WARP monitor, a computer with MASS and Event Manager, and a computer primarily dedicated to Internet access. The coordinator station receives all calls and passes them to the appropriate station. The coordinator has several manuals containing Standard Operating Procedures (SOPs) for handling different situations and to whom to delegate tasks in the field. The coordinator identifies an event site and who is responsible for the equipment there. The coordinator also monitors all eastern region Very High Frequency Omni-Directional Range Radars (VORs), all En Route Spacing Programs (ERMs), and all station generators, approximately 125 systems in all. The coordinator is responsible for the daily activity reports and has a direct line to the ATC System Command Center (ATCSCC) in Herndon. The coordinator has WARP running on one monitor, and was in almost continuous communication with field technicians, arranging for telecommunications agents to meet with FAA technicians at particular sites, among other things. The coordinator uses a system named Call Back to determine which personnel were responsible for which facilities. He uses Event Manager to record and view information relative to particular situations.

The monitor position interacts frequently with MASS and Event Manager. At this position, there were two monitors with different customized views of MASS. One monitor ran MASS only with 'time,' customized by the specialist, as the most important column of information. The other monitor interacted with both MASS and Event Manager. The monitor position was in phone communication to relay information on resets accomplished via MASS with different VORs almost constantly. This station also had a computer that updated message information and provided audible and visible alarms. The monitor was constantly fed information from the coordinator, the supervisor, and the scheduler who all had to field calls due to increased system volume on this severe weather day.

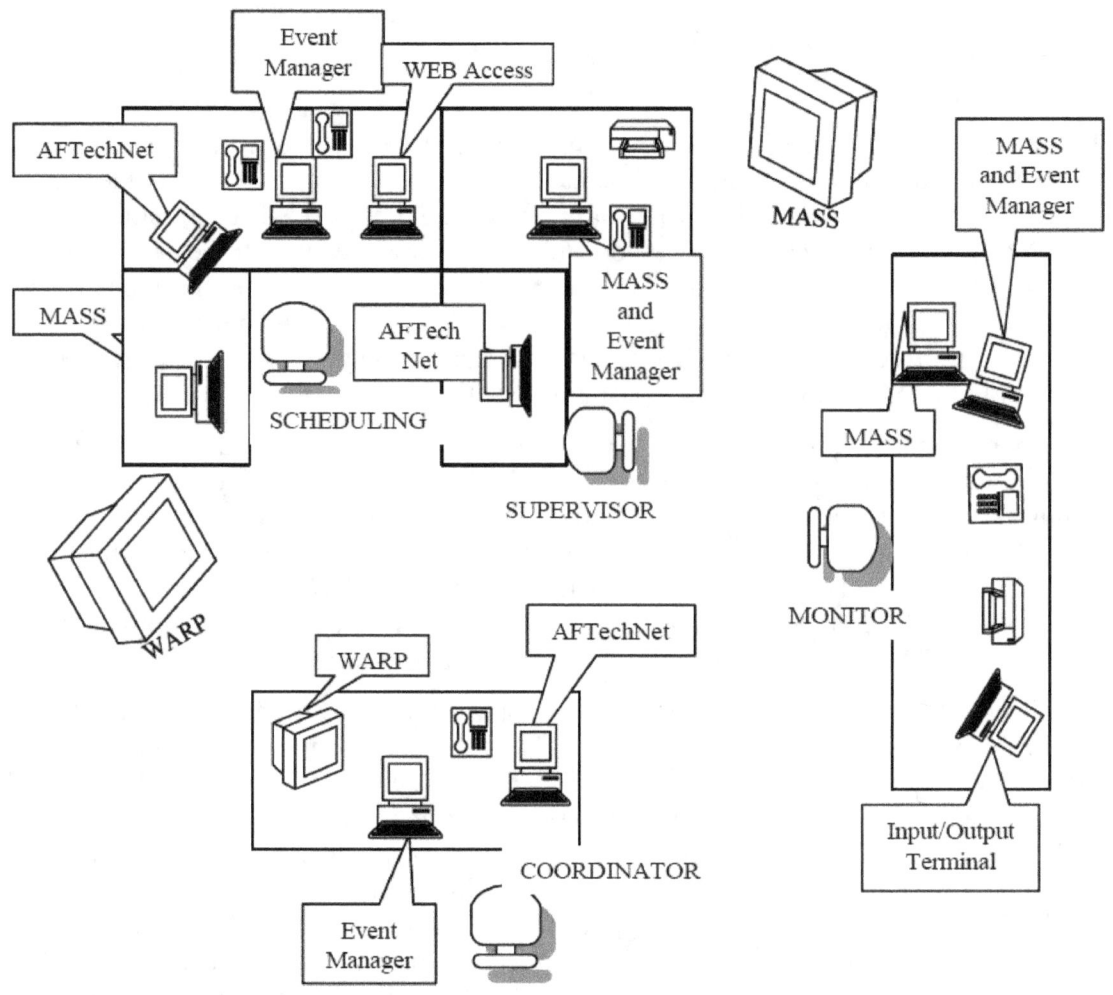

Washington Center – Leesburg, Va. GMCC

Figure 5. Leesburg GMCC Layout (approximately 30 ft x 25 ft).

Boston GMCC

The Boston GMCC is approximately 18 ft x 22 ft and is very well lighted. Seven specialists staff this facility in rotation 24/7. In general, there are three specialists on duty for the day shift, plus a supervisor. The specialists at this facility remain at their respective workstations. See Figure 6 for a layout of the Boston GMCC.

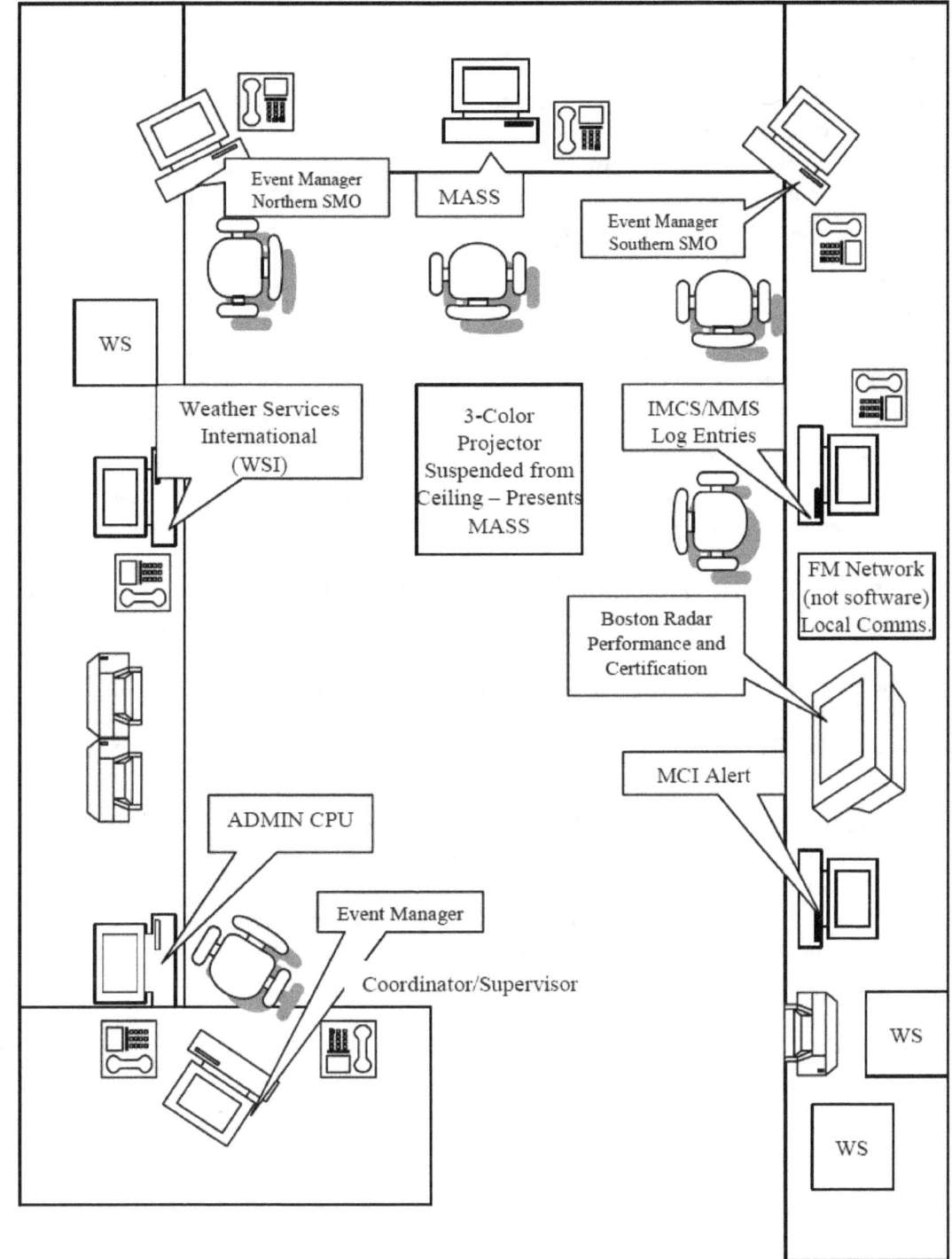

Boston Center – Logan International Airport Boston, Ma. GMCC

Figure 6. Boston GMCC Layout (approximately 18 ft x 22 ft).

As with the GMCC in Leesburg, there is a Coordinator work area, and most of the systems to be monitored and controlled are the same. There the similarities end. There are additional workstations with less formal position names: two of these run Event Manager most of the time (one for the Southern and one for the Northern System Management Offices), one station keeps MASS running all the time (in the center of the front of the area), and the final station is dedicated to RMM/Maintenance Monitoring System (MMS). This final station also includes an FM Network. This is not software; rather it is designed so the specialists can be in contact with the airport technical personnel via hand-held radio. Instead of WARP, the weather program used at the other facilities, at Boston GMCC, they have a software program named Weather Services International (WSI), Pilot Brief Vector. It is run on a small monitor (13 ft diagonal) near the coordinator/supervisor area. It provides detailed weather information and weather maps, similar to WARP. It is strictly to look at the weather (not maintenance and control of the system).

Additionally, there is one 36 in. TV that monitors the Logan International Airport radar. It is a system created by Dimensions International, and it is used to monitor radar performance and for certification of the specific Logan International Airport radar. There is an additional unique piece of software named MCI Alert created by MCI for the FAA. It provides direct information between the facility and MCI. It is similar to NetView software, which is the basis for HNL and HOCSR, and it provides color coding (Gray – normal, Yellow – minor, and Red – critical) and verbal alert signals. Finally, there is a three-color projector mounted to the ceiling, which presents MASS on the front wall of the work area. This allows personnel a large screen look at MASS. It is used primarily on the afternoon and night shifts, when only one or two specialists are on duty.

At the coordinator/supervisor workstation, there is an administrator Central Processing Unit (CPU). This allows administration level access to several systems including but not limited to Telecommunications Information Management System (TIMS), ProComm Plus for Windows (a dialing directory), and DynaComm/Elite, a program which has a compiler allowing the user to set color meaning in the system and change or set the meaning for the keys on the keyboard.

www.ingramcontent.com/pod-product-compliance
Lightning Source LLC
Chambersburg PA
CBHW080423290526
45791CB00008BA/2391